Endangered
Animals

VOLUME 4

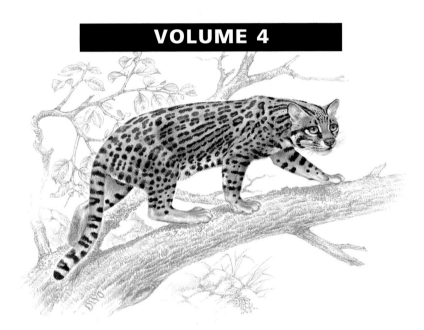

Darter, Watercress – **Frog,** Gastric-Brooding

GROLIER
EDUCATIONAL

Published 2002 by Grolier Educational, Danbury, CT 06816

This edition published exclusively for the school and library market

Produced by Andromeda Oxford Limited
11–13 The Vineyard, Abingdon,
Oxon OX14 3PX, U.K.
www.andromeda.co.uk

Principal Contributors: *Amy-Jane Beer, Andrew Campbell, Robert and Valerie Davies, John Dawes, Jonathan Elphick, Tim Halliday, Pat Morris. Further contributions by David Capper and John Woodward*

Project Director: *Graham Bateman*
Managing Editors: *Shaun Barrington, Jo Newson*
Editor: *Penelope Mathias*
Art Editor and Designer: *Steve McCurdy*
Cartographic Editor: *Tim Williams*
Editorial Assistant: *Marian Dreier*
Picture Manager: *Claire Turner*
Production: *Clive Sparling*
Indexers: *Indexing Specialists, Hove, East Sussex*

Reproduction by A. T. Color, Milan
Printing by H & Y Printing Ltd., Hong Kong

Set ISBN 0-7172-5584-0

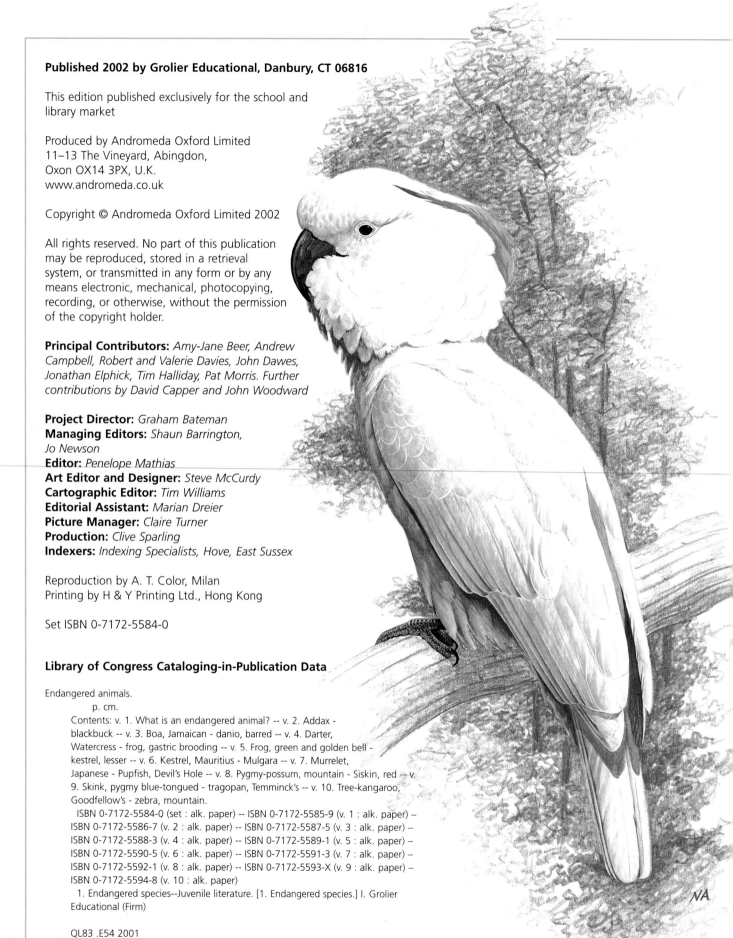

Library of Congress Cataloging-in-Publication Data

Endangered animals.
        p. cm.
        Contents: v. 1. What is an endangered animal? -- v. 2. Addax - blackbuck -- v. 3. Boa, Jamaican - danio, barred -- v. 4. Darter, Watercress - frog, gastric brooding -- v. 5. Frog, green and golden bell - kestrel, lesser -- v. 6. Kestrel, Mauritius - Mulgara -- v. 7. Murrelet, Japanese - Pupfish, Devil's Hole -- v. 8. Pygmy-possum, mountain - Siskin, red -- v. 9. Skink, pygmy blue-tongued - tragopan, Temminck's -- v. 10. Tree-kangaroo, Goodfellow's - zebra, mountain.
        ISBN 0-7172-5584-0 (set : alk. paper) -- ISBN 0-7172-5585-9 (v. 1 : alk. paper) –
        ISBN 0-7172-5586-7 (v. 2 : alk. paper) -- ISBN 0-7172-5587-5 (v. 3 : alk. paper) –
        ISBN 0-7172-5588-3 (v. 4 : alk. paper) -- ISBN 0-7172-5589-1 (v. 5 : alk. paper) –
        ISBN 0-7172-5590-5 (v. 6 : alk. paper) -- ISBN 0-7172-5591-3 (v. 7 : alk. paper) –
        ISBN 0-7172-5592-1 (v. 8 : alk. paper) -- ISBN 0-7172-5593-X (v. 9 : alk. paper) –
        ISBN 0-7172-5594-8 (v. 10 : alk. paper)
        1. Endangered species--Juvenile literature. [1. Endangered species.] I. Grolier Educational (Firm)

QL83 .E54 2001
333.95'42--dc21   00-069134

Contents

About This Set

Endangered Animals is a 10-volume set that highlights and explains the threats to animal species across the world. Habitat loss is one major threat; another is the introduction of species into areas where they do not normally live.

Examples of different animals facing a range of problems have been chosen to include all the major animal groups. Fish, reptiles, amphibians, and insects and invertebrates are included as well as mammals and birds. Some species may have very large populations, but they nevertheless face problems. Some are already extinct.

Volume 1—What Is an Endangered Animal?—explains how scientists classify animals, the reasons why they are endangered, and what conservationists are doing about it. Cross-references in the text (volume number followed by page number) show relevant pages in the set.

Volumes 2 to 10 contain individual species entries arranged in alphabetical order. Each entry is a double-page spread with a data panel summarizing key facts and a locator map showing its range.

Look for a particular species by its common name, listed in alphabetical order on the Contents page of each book. (Page references for both common and scientific names are in the full set index at the back of each book.) When you have found the species that interests you, you can find related entries by looking first in the data panel. If an animal listed under Related endangered species has an asterisk (*) next to its name, it has its own separate entry. You can also check the cross-references at the bottom of the left-hand page, which refer to entries in other volumes. (For example, "Finch, Gouldian 4: 74" means that the two-page entry about the Gouldian finch starts on page 74 of Volume 4.) The cross-reference is usually made to an animal that is in the same genus or family as the species you are reading about; but a species may appear here because it is from the same part of the world or faces the same threats.

Each book ends with a glossary of terms, lists of useful publications and websites, and a full set index.

Darter, Watercress

Etheostoma nuchale

To us watercress is a leafy, spicy plant we add to salads. To the watercress darter it is the difference between survival and extinction. So called because of its intimate association with a few watercress-rich springs in Jefferson County, Alabama, this little fish is in need of protection.

Only a handful of fish species have been declared Endangered within a few years of discovery. The gold sawfin goodeid (**5**: 36) is one of them; the watercress darter is another.

Precarious Habitat

The watercress darter was discovered at Glenn Springs in Bessemer, Jefferson County, Alabama, in 1964. Over the following years searches mounted in other springs in the area failed to yield any further specimens, leading scientists to conclude that Glenn Springs held the only population of the species.

While this in itself would have formed a strong argument for listing the watercress darter as under extreme threat, it was the added factors of location of the site, its size, and the high risk of pollution that led to its official listing just six years after its discovery.

Contrary to common (but mistaken) belief, type localities for species, whether they are endangered or otherwise, are not always exotic or remote areas. In the case of the watercress darter, for example, Glenn Springs, the small site where it was discovered—and to which it was believed to be restricted—is no more than than 60 feet (18 m) away from a busy highway. One chemical spillage could therefore easily wipe out the whole population overnight. The establishment of shopping complexes and apartments with their drainage and sewerage services directs essential rainwater away from the land and into drains, depriving natural watercourses of their seasonal renewal. As a result, water levels drop, sometimes to the point where habitats dry up.

Subsequent Discoveries and Threats

Shortly after the high-risk status of Glenn Springs was established, a Watercress Darter Recovery Team was set up by the U.S. Fish and Wildlife Service through its Office of Endangered Species.

The first and most urgent challenge was to establish whether the watercress darter occurred anywhere else apart from the original locality. To the team's great relief extensive searches revealed its presence in two other water bodies: Thomas's Spring and Roebuck Springs. Relief was tempered with concern, however, since water samples

DATA PANEL

Watercress darter

Etheostoma nuchale

Family: Percidae

World population: About 19,000 specimens (mid- to late 1980s estimate); no current figures available

Distribution: Known from only 3 springs in Jefferson County, Alabama: Glenn Springs, Thomas's Spring, and Roebuck Springs

Habitat: Heavily vegetated pools and runs in which the dominant plants include watercress, the filamentous alga *Spirogyra*, and *Chara*

Size: About 2.1 in (5.4 cm), but up to 2.5 in (6.4 cm) reported

Form: Fusiform (spindle-shaped) or slightly compressed body with 2 dorsal (back) fins. Males have bright

orange-red bellies and blue and orange fins during the breeding season; females are less brightly colored

Diet: Mainly small aquatic snails, crustaceans, and insects

Breeding: The season is believed to be March–July; few details are known

Related endangered Species: 22 other species of *Etheostoma* are listed by IUCN; Maryland darter (*E. sellore*) is Extinct

Status: IUCN EN; not listed by CITES

See also: Pollution **1**: 50; Introductions **1**: 54; Sunfish, Spring Pygmy **9**: 40

that were sent for testing revealed a degree of bacterial contamination that was far greater than was considered safe.

In Glenn Springs, for instance, the tests showed that coliform bacterial contamination was 350 per 100 milliliters of water. To put this into perspective, a count of 4 per 100 milliliters is thought to indicate significant contamination. Roebuck Springs water was worse. Tests over 10 years had produced counts of between 440 and 3,600 per 100 milliliters.

Thomas's Spring did not show any such contamination, so it seemed a good habitat for the darter. And so it proved to be—until the grass carp *Ctenopharyngodon idella* was introduced to clear the pool of vegetation. The grass carp deprived the watercress darter of essential cover and its food: the aquatic invertebrates that lived among the watercress.

Recovery Status

In 1980 Thomas's Spring, which had been privately owned, was acquired by the U.S. Fish and Wildlife Service and became the Watercress Darter National Wildlife Refuge. The grass carp were removed, and the spring gradually became revegetated. The watercress darter began to reestablish itself, probably from the small population that had survived downstream from the main pool and hence away from the area that had suffered intense grazing from the introduced grass carp. Although some natural predators, such as sunfish, exist at this site, the thick vegetation cover offers the watercress darter good protection, and the population seems to be increasing.

The situation at Roebuck Springs is not quite so favorable. Here the high level of pollution, caused

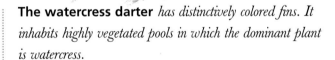

The watercress darter *has distinctively colored fins. It inhabits highly vegetated pools in which the dominant plant is watercress.*

largely by sewage seepage, produces high nitrogen concentrations in the water. They are affecting the watercress darter population, some 50 percent of which are now suffering from "gas bubble disease," and the population is believed to be decreasing.

Pollution also seems to be affecting the Glenn Springs population, although no incidences of the disease have been detected. There are reports that two of the several small populations of watercress darters that have been introduced into apparently suitable "transplant" sites have disappeared, although some others are reported to be doing well. Despite these successes, however, the position of the watercress darter is still precarious.

5

Deer, Chinese Water

Hydropotes inermis

Originally occupying areas of Korea and the Yangtze River Basin in China, the Chinese water deer has been introduced to England and France. The European deer populations are now more secure than their Asian relatives, which are threatened by development, shooting, and trapping.

The Chinese water deer lives in the swamps of eastern central China; a separate subspecies is found in similar habitats in Korea. Although water deer frequent reed beds and wet places, they prefer dry land.

Unlike many deer, Chinese water deer live alone and do not form herds, although some may remain together as small family groups. Males defend their territories vigorously, especially during the winter mating season. Rival males stand side by side and try to use their tusks (they do not have antlers) to inflict serious wounds on each other.

The deer are active mainly at dusk and dawn, hiding away in dense vegetation for the rest of the day. Water deer can swim well and often do so in order to reach feeding or resting places on islands or across rivers. Their digestion is relatively inefficient, so they must select their food carefully, avoiding coarse fibrous materials. When frightened, water deer make a loud bark and leap away in high bounds.

Multiple Threats

In China the deer are frequently trapped as pests, since they raid crops. However, they are also considered valuable because the female's colostrum (a thin, milky secretion produced by the mother for the first few days after her young are born, before true lactation begins) is believed to have medicinal properties. Killing the mother to obtain the substance results in the death of offspring as well.

The deer are also threatened by development. As more and more land is taken up by farms, roads, and towns, people have squeezed out many wild animals.

DATA PANEL

Chinese water deer

Hydropotes inermis

Family: Cervidae

World population: Thousands, but reliable estimates not available

Distribution: Yangtze River Basin in China; Korea; introduced to Britain and France

Habitat: Reed beds in wet places; also dry land

Size: Length head/body: 3–3.5 ft (90–95 cm); tail: 2 in (6.5 cm); height: 18–22 in (45–55 cm). Weight: 30–35 lb (14–16 kg)

Form: Small, golden-brown deer with white belly. Face short and rounded. Sleek and slender in summer, but more thickset appearance in winter, owing to long, dense coat. Fur stiff and bristly with hollow, brittle hairs that break easily. Prominent tusks in male, but no antlers. Young are dark brown with white spots and stripes

Diet: Mostly sedges (grasslike plants); also reeds, flowers, and shrubs such as brambles

Breeding: Breeds when only a few months old; usually 1 or 2 young per family, but up to 4 possible; born May–July. May live up to 12 years

Related endangered species: Kuhl's deer *(Axis kuhlii)** EN; Père David's deer *(Elaphurus davidianus)** CR

Status: IUCN LRnt; not listed by CITES

See also: Introductions **1:** 54; Deer, Kuhl's **4:** 8; Deer, Père David's **4:** 10

In 1990 there were estimated to be only about 10,000 water deer left in China. The status of those in Korea is unknown, but the animals are unlikely to be any more secure. The decline is partly a result of recent famines in North Korea, when many forms of wildlife were eaten by humans. However, water deer breed well in captivity; a few were released in central France in 1954 and are still present in the wild.

Escape into the Wild

There are also wild Chinese water deer in Britain originating from a captive herd in Woburn Park (Bedfordshire) in southern central England. In the 1890s animals brought from China by the Duke of Bedford bred successfully, and soon there were more than 100 of them. Some were transferred to the nearby Whipsnade wild animal park in 1929. They too did well, and many escaped into the surrounding countryside, where their numbers increased. In about 1950 water deer were deliberately released on the fens (lowlying flat land) of Cambridgeshire in eastern England, where several hundred now live. Altogether, Britain now has more than 1,000 water deer. The mild winters of recent years have allowed better survival of the young, so numbers have continued to increase.

Since they do little harm and have few predators, the British population seems secure and is perhaps in less danger than the original Chinese population. Their success poses a dilemma because introduced species often become pests and, by international agreement, are supposed to be eliminated in their nonnative countries. However, perhaps the Chinese water deer living in Britain should be left alone in case the native Asian populations become even more seriously endangered in the future.

The Chinese water deer *has coarse, brittle hair that breaks easily, leaving patches resembling scars.*

Deer, Kuhl's

Axis kuhlii

The rare, shy Kuhl's deer is restricted to the tiny Indonesian island of Bawean, where it is more often heard than seen and is difficult to study. Most information on Kuhl's deer has been gleaned from captive specimens.

Kuhl's deer is the world's least widespread species of deer. It lives only on the tiny Indonesian island of Bawean in the middle of the Java Sea. The deer keep mostly to the patchy forests of the western half of the island, which, despite being widely cultivated, offer enough wild, dense vegetation to keep the deer well hidden and provide them with adequate food. Under ideal conditions Kuhl's deer come out to feed at dusk and dawn, but when they live close to human habitation, they tend to become fully nocturnal.

Although the total population probably numbers no more than 400 individuals, Kuhl's deer are concentrated in such a small area that the population density is misleadingly high—estimated at about

36 per square mile (15 per sq. km). The fact that they are so rarely seen, even by Bawean Island people who live and work close by, is testament to their shy and retiring nature. Kuhl's deer rarely venture far out into the open; instead, they barge their way through undergrowth, head down, in a crouching, skulking posture; their stooping stance is caused by their front legs being slightly shorter than their back ones.

Both males and females are stocky animals, with long, barrel-shaped bodies and short legs. While certainly not built for running, Kuhl's deer are capable of brief bursts of speed and will sprint for cover if they are caught out in the open. However, as soon as the immediate threat has passed, they will revert to their preferred creeping gait.

Breeding

Most accounts of the lifestyle of Kuhl's deer are based on captive specimens kept in several zoos around the world. The deer have an extended breeding season, which lasts from July to November. Nevertheless, most matings take place in September and October, resulting in a peak number of births in May or June. Males in breeding condition will stamp and bark at rivals in an attempt to prove their strength without resorting to violence, but fights break out quite frequently. The bucks have short antlers, usually with three points, called tines, which they use in combat. For most of the year both males and females live on their own,

DATA PANEL

Kuhl's deer (Bawean deer)

Axis kuhlii

Family: Cervidae

World population: About 400

Distribution: Bawean Island, Indonesia

Habitat: Deciduous forest and clearings

Size: Length head/body: 40–44 in (105–115 cm); height at shoulder: up to 25 in (70 cm). Weight: 80–110 lb (36–50 kg)

Form: Long-bodied deer with distinctive crouching posture. Coat uniformly brown with dark stripe along back. Large black nose, large dark eyes accentuated by rings of pale fur. Males have 3-pointed antlers

Diet: Grass, flowers, shoots, and leaves

Breeding: Single young born February–June after a gestation of about 10 months. Life span up to 15 years

Related endangered species: Various deer, including Père David's deer *(Elaphurus davidianus)** CR

Status: IUCN EN; CITES I

Borneo

INDONESIA
◉ Bawean

Java
Bali
Sumbawa

See also: Island Biogeography **1:** 30; Deer, Chinese Water **4:** 6; Deer, Père David's **4:** 10

Kuhl's deer *has a slightly crouching appearance due to its front legs being shorter than its back legs.*

communicating by short, sharp barks. The breeding season is the only time that the deer actively seek each other's company. Only mothers with young live side by side for any length of time. It takes about six months for the young deer to be fully weaned onto the adult diet of grasses, shoots, leaves, and flowers.

Vulnerable Island Species

People cannot be held entirely responsible for the decline of an animal that has a very limited range. It is a sad fact that species from small and remote islands are far more vulnerable to environmental pressures than their continental counterparts. Whole island populations can be be affected by relatively small-scale events; a single outbreak of disease or a localized environmental disaster, for example, could result in extinction.

In recent years, however, a large proportion of the local economy on the island of Bawean has been generated through teak plantations. The island is widely cultivated, and the appropriation of land for plantations has increased pressure on the deer's natural habitat and put their future in serious doubt.

Deer, Père David's

Elaphurus davidianus

Extinct in the wild for centuries, this species has survived only in parks and zoos. It is now being reintroduced into special reserves in its native China.

The unusual-looking Père David's deer is called "four-unlike" in Chinese, a reference to its peculiar appearance. It seems to have the antlers of a deer, broad hooves like those of a cow, a neck like that of a camel, and the long bushy tail of a donkey; yet it is also quite distinct in its appearance.

Its habitat used to be the swampy lowlands of eastern and central China. It was hunted to extinction over most of its range more than 800 years ago, though some may have survived until the 19th century on Hainan Island in the South China Sea. Meanwhile, a few were kept by the emperor in the secluded Imperial Hunting Park of Peking (Beijing), protected by armed guards and contained within a high wall over 40 miles (64 km) long. There, in 1865, the French missionary Father Armand David saw them, and he later managed to obtain two skins that he thought were from some sort of reindeer. They were studied in Europe and described in 1866 as a new species of deer. They were named after Father David.

News of the curious creatures reached the outside world, including the Duke of Bedford in England, who was particularly interested in deer. He arranged for some living specimens to be brought to his collection at Woburn Park (about 60 miles (96 km) northwest of London). The Chinese emperor also allowed some to be sent to France and Germany. The export of animals was extremely fortunate, since in 1895 massive floods destroyed part of the Imperial Hunting Park's wall. Many deer drowned; those that escaped were killed and eaten by hungry people in the surrounding countryside. About two dozen seem to have survived within the park, but they were killed and eaten by soldiers during the Boxer Rebellion in 1900.

All the deer alive today are derived from those few that had been taken to Europe. The Duke of Bedford arranged for animals to be gathered together from various zoos to add to his collection and to form a breeding group at Woburn. The herd suffered through the two world wars due to the shortage of food, but numbers steadily increased; by 1956 there were sufficient numbers to be able to send four animals to the Beijing zoo. Today the largest herd is still at Woburn, where there are about 600 to 700 animals. Another sizable herd is at Wadhurst in Sussex (in the south of England), with smaller numbers in parks and zoos around the world.

Narrow Escape

In 1985, 22 deer were sent from Woburn as a gift to the people of China. They were returned to a small 100-acre (40-ha) enclosure in part of the original Imperial Hunting Park. Another 39 animals were sent from British zoos in 1986 and released in the Da Feng Reserve 250 miles (380 km) north of Shanghai. It is a marshy coastal area, the sort of habitat originally favored by Père David's deer and within its former range. The deer bred well, and numbers have tripled within 10 years.

Fortunately, Père David's deer does not seem to be badly affected by inbreeding, despite the small gene pool from which modern populations are descended. The species has had a narrow escape from extinction; and although its total population remains small, it does seem to be secure as a semicaptive animal.

Père David's deer *are unique in that the front prongs of their antlers are branched.*

See also: National Parks **1:** 92; Deer, Chinese Water **4:** 6; Deer, Kuhl's **4:** 8; Deer, Siberian Musk **4:** 12

DATA PANEL

Père David's deer

Elaphurus davidianus

Family: Cervidae

World population: About 1,000–1,500

Distribution: Originally northeastern and east central China, and on Hainan Island until the 19th century. Now only in special reserves in China and zoos and parks in various countries

Habitat: Swampy lowlands

Size: Length: male 6–6.3 ft (1.8–1.9 m); tail: 24 in (60 cm); height at shoulder: male 45–48 in (114–122 cm); female slightly smaller. Weight: male 330–440 lb (150–200 kg); female about 20% lighter

Form: Resembling other deer. Coat is gray in winter, reddish brown in summer. The tail is long for a deer, with a black tip. The males have a shaggy mane. The antlers are heavy and unique in that the front prongs are branched

Diet: Grass and leaves; sometimes aquatic plants

Breeding: One young born per year; mature at 14 months. Life span up to 20 years

Related endangered species: Various other species of deer, including Kuhl's deer *(Axis kuhlii)** EN

Status: IUCN CR; not listed by CITES

CHINA NORTH KOREA SOUTH KOREA

Deer, Siberian Musk

Moschus moschiferus

Siberian musk deer are small, solitary, mountain-dwelling creatures that have been ruthlessly hunted for their musk—a highly valued ingredient in medicines and perfumes.

The Siberian musk deer lives alone, not in herds. It is small in stature and inhabits forests in mountain regions from Siberia to the Himalayas. The deer are mainly nocturnal, coming into the open to feed at night. In summer they may travel to higher altitudes to feed, retreating when the snows begin in the fall. However, individuals rarely travel far during their normal activities. Musk deer have a keen sense of hearing, and the males are strongly territorial.

The deer have large ears and a short tail. Neither sex has antlers, but males have sharp, downward-pointing tusks (canine teeth) that are often more than 4 inches (10 cm) long.

Like many animals that live in dense undergrowth, musk deer rely heavily on scent to leave messages for others of their species, since it is impossible to see for any distance. They smear the scent on to rocks and logs, and it is also deposited with droppings and urine. Musk—one of the scents—is produced only by the males. Sexually mature males produce the musk from a pocket on the belly, and it probably serves to attract potential mates.

Worth its Weight...

A brownish, waxy substance, musk was widely believed to have important healing properties and was used for medicinal purposes in Europe and Asia. Later it became a component of high-quality perfumes and soaps, although nowadays a synthetic substitute can be used. Up to 1 ounce (28 g) of musk could be extracted from a single animal, and although musk can be taken from a living animal, it was easier to

DATA PANEL

Siberian musk deer

Moschus moschiferus

Family: Moschidae

World population: About 100,000, but spread over a huge area

Distribution: Siberia, Manchuria, Korea, China, and Sakhalin Island; some in Mongolia

Habitat: Mountain forests up to 5,000 ft (1,600 m) above sea level

Size: Length: 30–36 in (76.2–91 cm); height: 20–21 in (50–55 cm); males often smaller than females. Weight: 24–30 lb (11–14 kg)

Form: Hind legs longer than forelegs, so the rump is higher than the shoulders, and the back appears arched. The coat is spotted when young, but adults are a dark grayish brown. They have no antlers. Males have sharp canine teeth that project downward as tusks

Diet: Mostly lichens, but also leaves, conifer needles, and tree bark. In summer a wide range of small herbaceous plants; also some grasses

Breeding: Breeding season November–December; 1 or (rarely) 2 young born in June of the following year. Can live up to 20 years in captivity

Related endangered species: Forest musk deer *(Moschus berezovskii)* LRnt; black musk deer *(M. fuscus)* LRnt; *M. chrysogaster* (no common name) LRnt

Status: IUCN VU; CITES I and II, according to country location

See also: Hunting 1: 42; Deer, Chinese Water 4: 6; Deer, Père David's 4: 10; Whale, Sperm (see text on ambergris) 10: 56

Siberian musk deer *have no antlers. The male (left) has long, downward-pointing canine teeth, and the young have a spotted coat (right).*

shoot the deer than capture them alive. The extract fetched high prices, sometimes as much as its own weight in gold. The golf-ball sized pouch in which the musk is contained was also considered valuable. In one year over 100,000 glands were imported into Japan; in another more than 80,000 were exported from Russia to China. Nowadays international trade is prohibited, but black market activities continue.

It is thought that more than 5,000 male musk deer are killed every year. The females do not produce musk, but it is hard to avoid killing them by mistake, so populations are reduced. As a result of hunting, the species has already become extinct in some areas, and the total population is thought to have halved during

the 1990s. Predators, particularly lynx, take many deer, especially the young as they lie beneath the dense foliage of fir trees in early summer. Added to this, forests have been cleared for timber and fuel, and to make way for farmland, grazing animals, and roads. There is still enough of the habitat left to support several hundred thousand musk deer, but the numbers are declining.

Siberian musk deer do not breed well in captivity, so farming them cannot satisfy the demand for musk. Catching wild deer to remove the musk and then releasing them is also not very successful, and both activities encourage continued trade in musk. While this goes on, every musk deer is at risk.

Desman, Russian

Desmana moschata

The Russian desman—an amphibious relative of the mole—has been hunted extensively for its fur. It has also suffered as a result of water pollution and from competition with introduced species.

Desmans were once widespread across Europe, and fossils have been found as far west as Britain. However, only two species now exist: one that is found in the Pyrenees mountains of northern Spain and Portugal, with a few in southwestern France, and the other in European Russia and the Ukraine. The Pyrenean desman is classified as Vulnerable. Its population size is unknown (probably low thousands) and is declining.

Little is known about the basic biology and social organization of the desman. It is an amphibious mammal that gets more than half of its food from hunting in water. The Pyrenean desman seems to be a solitary creature with a small, permanent home range. It prefers cool lakes and fast-flowing rivers. In places it lives at altitudes of more than 5,500 feet (1,800 m). The Pyrenean desman suffers badly when rivers dry up as a result of water extraction for agricultural use, especially in warmer areas where water flow may be severely reduced during the summer.

Unlike the Pyrenean desman, the Russian desman appears to be nomadic, although it has been recorded living in shared burrows. Its preferred habitat is lakes and slow-flowing water. Desmans build their burrows among the waterside vegetation in which they hunt for food, but they also use the water plants as camouflage to hide from predators.

Hunted to Extinction

Like mink and muskrats, desmans have a coat that has dense, soft underfur and long, glossy "guard" hairs. This two-layer coat effectively insulates the animals from the cold water, but also provides a superb fur for fashionable garments. Russian desman numbers were severely affected by hunting during the 19th century because of the value of the silky coat. Hundreds of thousands of desmans were killed for the fur trade: In just two years over 300,000 skins were sold to China, and at the beginning of the 20th century about 20,000 skins were being processed each year.

Since desmans rarely travel far from water, traps set along river banks and lake shores were an effective

DATA PANEL

Russian desman

Desmana moschata

Family: Talpidae

World population: About 40,000

Distribution: River systems of the Don, Ural, and Volga in southwestern Russia and the Ukraine

Habitat: Permanently wet habitats, river edges, lakes, and marshes

Size: Length head/body: 7–9 in (18–22 cm); tail: 7–8.5 in (17–21.5 cm). Weight: 1.75–3.5 oz (50–100 g)

Form: Ratlike mammal with long, flexible nose and long, glossy hair. Tail scaly and flattened from side to side; partially webbed feet. Various parts of body have sensory whiskers

Diet: Aquatic insects, mollusks, fish, and frogs

Breeding: Families of 3–5 young produced twice per year. Life span unknown, probably 2–3 years

Related endangered species: Pyrenean desman *(Galemys pyrenaicus)* VU

Status: IUCN VU; not listed by CITES

See also: Drainage and Irrigation **1:** 40; Introductions **1:** 54; Solenodon, Cuban **9:** 16; Tenrec, Aquatic **9:** 64

method of capture. If trapping persisted for any length of time, the entire population could be wiped out locally. Fishermen setting nets to catch small fish often captured desmans as well and may sometimes have done so deliberately. The desmans represented a valuable addition to the normal catch.

Once the Russian desman had been officially recognized as rare in 1929, it was given legal protection, and most trapping ended. However, other threats loomed. Hydroelectric projects affected water flow and therefore the suitability of the habitat for both the desman and its diet of aquatic invertebrates. Habitat disturbance forced desmans to move on, seeking new places in which to live and feed. In addition, grazing farm animals and riverside development removed the vegetation from long stretches of bank, taking away the desman's refuges and leading to their local extinction. A further threat has come from introduced rodents such as the muskrat (from North America) and the coypu (from South America). Kept on fur farms, they were released or escaped into the desman's home waters. They have competed for burrows and shelter, eaten waterside plants, and successfully displaced the smaller desman.

Water quality has been affected by industrial and agricultural pollution. The influx of nutrients—particularly as a result of fertilizer runoff from farmland—encourages the growth of algae. The algae multiply, using all the oxygen and turning the water into a dense green "soup." The lack of oxygen also kills insects and crustaceans, the main food of desmans.

Recently conservationists have captured and released over 10,000 Russian desmans into places where competition and pollution threats are less serious. The animals have also been reintroduced to parts of their range where they had become extinct. Reintroduction only works where the original threat (hunting) is being controlled, and the habitat remains suitable. There are now special refuges set aside to protect surviving desman populations, but numbers are still declining.

The desman *is adapted for foraging in water. It has partially webbed feet and extrasensitive whiskers on the muzzle. It also has hypersensitive hairs on its tail and legs, and its nostrils and ears can be closed by valves.*

Dhole

Cuon alpinus

Centuries of intensive persecution and habitat destruction on a massive scale have taken their toll on this unusual wild dog, whose fascinating daily life has only recently been studied.

The highly adaptable dhole was once relatively common throughout a vast range that covered much of southern Russia, Mongolia, China, India, and Southeast Asia to Java. Like many other wild canids (members of the dog family), the dhole has suffered from severe prejudice.

Until quite recently the dhole could be killed with impunity throughout its range. To be fair, the species' dreadful reputation did have some basis in fact. Anyone who has witnessed a dhole kill could be forgiven for concluding that they are indeed wanton and unnecessarily cruel killers. Unlike most predators, which dispatch their prey with a fatal bite to the throat or spinal cord, dholes kill by ripping open the victim's belly, often beginning to eat well before the animal has bled to death. If such a kill is disturbed by people watching, the dholes retreat, and the victim may take even longer to die. It is easy enough to understand why a farmer or tribesman coming across such a scene of carnage—especially if it involved one of their own cattle or goats—would want to eliminate the dhole from the neighborhood.

Doting Dads

There is, however, another side to the dhole's nature. Like the painted hunting dog of Africa or the Amazonian bush dog, the dhole lives and hunts in packs that are models of cooperation and tolerance.

Within a pack the majority of individuals are male. Only one female in the group will breed, and the rest of the pack make it their business to protect and serve her family. When the pups are very young, the pack restricts its range to the region of the den, often leaving one of its number to stand guard over the precious family. The pack visits regularly, bringing food for the mother and her offspring. The pups will start eating regurgitated meat from the age of about three weeks. Later, when the youngsters are old enough to begin following the pack on hunting excursions, their doting relatives not only keep a close eye on them to ensure their safety, but they will also allow them first access to any kill. Dholes tend not to fight over food—each dog ensures its fair share by simply eating as fast as it can—and the pack hierarchy means that there is rarely any dispute over the right to mate.

Misunderstood

All in all, dholes are fascinating and misunderstood animals for whom the tide of opinion has just begun to turn. Even so, it is unlikely that the dhole will ever be popular with local people. There is no escaping the fact that they can and do kill livestock and game, and will continue to do so.

Past generations of dholes have been shot, snared, and poisoned. Now that the species is protected, such killings are illegal, but there is little doubt that they still take place. The greatest concern at present is over the status of two of the three Indian subspecies of dhole; the Himalayan and trans-Himalayan dholes are both thought to be on the verge of extinction. Numbers of the third Indian subspecies—the peninsular dhole—have rallied a little. Their small recovery is thanks largely to the establishment of nature reserves and national parks intended to protect the tiger. Elsewhere in their range, dholes are surviving in ever-smaller fragments of habitat, often in very poor and remote areas where it is difficult for the authorities to enforce any ban on hunting.

See also: Pasture 1: 38; Hunting 1: 42; Dog, African Wild 4: 22; Dog, Bush 4: 24; Wolf, Gray 10: 68

DATA PANEL

Dhole (Asian wild dog, red dog)

Cuon alpinus

Family: Canidae

World population: Unknown

Distribution: Western Asia to China, India, and Malay Peninsula; Sumatra and Java

Habitat: Forest, wooded hill, and steppe; often rests in clearings but rarely seen in very large open spaces

Size: Length: up to 36 in (92 cm); height at shoulder: up to 20 in (50 cm). Weight: 37–44 lb (17–20 kg)

Form: Robust, collie-sized dog with light grayish-brown to rich-red coat and dark bushy tail; muzzle short and powerful; one fewer molar teeth than other canids

Diet: Insects, reptiles, and other mammals of any size up to large stag; occasionally berries and other fruit

Breeding: Litters of about 8 pups born November–March after 9-week gestation; mature after 1 year. Typical longevity unknown

Related endangered species: Red wolf (*Canis rufus*)* CR; Ethiopian wolf (*C. simensis*)* CR; African wild dog (*Lycaon pictus*)* EN

Status: IUCN VU; CITES II

The dhole
is a seemingly brutal killer but also a cooperative family carer.

17

Dipper, Rufous-Throated

Cinclus schulzi

The little-known rufous-throated dipper is a specialized river- and stream-dweller that is threatened in its limited, fragmented range by declines in water quality.

Birds in the small family Cinclidae, which are known as dippers, have a wide distribution in temperate and cooler subtropical regions, but only within a restricted habitat. They are remarkable in being the only passerines (perching birds) to be truly aquatic, living only on and around streams and rivers. Thought to be closely related to thrushes, dippers probably originated in North America and later spread westward to Eurasia and southward to Central and South America.

In South America two closely related species are found. The strikingly patterned white-capped dipper occurs from mountains in Colombia and Venezuela, south to northwestern Bolivia. The more subtly plumaged rufous-throated dipper—until recently often thought to be a race of the white-capped dipper—is the rarest of dippers. It has a patchy and local distribution only on the eastern slopes of the Andes in southern Bolivia and northwestern Argentina.

Aquatic Life

The rufous-throated dipper prefers fast-flowing water fringed with rocky banks or cliffs that have waterfalls, torrents, and rocks, while at the same time containing stable channels. Such precise habitat requirements are related to the bird's feeding and breeding habits.

Unlike the other dipper species, the two South American species rarely swim or dive underwater to walk along the stream or riverbed in search of food. Instead, they stand on the edge of a waterfall or cascade and pluck prey from the rocks with their bill, often being briefly submerged in

DATA PANEL

Rufous-throated dipper

Cinclus schulzi

Family: Cinclidae

World population: 3,000–4,000 birds (estimated)

Distribution: A small region of northwestern Argentina and southern Bolivia on the eastern slopes of the Andean mountains

Habitat: Breeds along fast-flowing, rocky rivers and streams mainly where alder trees fringe the banks; descends to larger, slower-flowing rivers during periods of frost

Size: Length: 6 in (15 cm)

Form: Plump-bodied bird with large head, usually hunched; sloping back; short, rounded wings; short tail; sturdy legs and feet; plumage mainly dark, dull slate-gray with paler gray chin, pale pinkish-rufous

throat; white patch on the inner edges of the primary flight feathers of each wing visible in flight or when the bird flicks its wings

Diet: Limited observations indicate that it consists mainly of aquatic insects, such as caddis and blackfly larvae and mayfly nymphs

Breeding: Little known. Nests in crevices on cliffs or banks, or among boulders September–January. Nests examined were very like those of other dipper species, with a bulky outer globular shell of mosses, grass stems, rootlets, and green algae and an entrance at the side, with an inner cup of grass stems, green algae, alder leaves, and sometimes pieces of paper or plastic

Related endangered species: No other species of dippers are threatened

Status: IUCN VU; not listed by CITES

See also: Specialization 1: 28; Drainage and Irrigation 1: 40; Manakin, Black-Capped 6: 66; Siskin, Red 8: 94

the rushing water. In less turbulent stretches they wade in the water up to their bellies and probe among boulders and stones for prey.

Rufous-throated dippers are usually found on their own or as pairs. They are strongly territorial, each pair defending a narrow, linear territory along the stream or river. They seem to prefer spending the breeding season at altitudes of about 4,900 to 8,200 feet (1,500 to 2,500 m) in cloud forest characterized by alder trees growing along the streams and rivers, but they have also been recorded above and below this zone and on streams in pastureland, where they may also breed. In frosty periods the birds descend to larger rivers at altitudes of about 2,600 feet (800 m).

Declining Population

Estimates of the population in Bolivia range from a possible 500 pairs to a probable 1,000 pairs, while in Argentina figures suggest that only 1,000 pairs survive. The bird is found only in some localities, and each subpopulation seems to be extremely small, so the threats to its habitat are potentially very serious.

In many parts of its range, especially in Bolivia, the places where it lives are still remote, sparsely populated, and relatively inaccessible. Nevertheless, some river systems, especially in Argentina, are affected by a range of developments. They include the building of reservoirs, irrigation projects, and hydroelectric dams, which result in

reduced water flow, alteration of river channels, and pollution, particularly at lower levels. Eutrophication—overenrichment by nutrients, particularly nitrates and phosphates—due to runoff from fertilizers or discharged waste, has also affected rivers in Argentina, leading to an abundance of algae, which reduces the availability of the dipper's insect food.

Along other stretches of water, woodland is adversely affected by logging or livestock grazing, resulting in soil erosion. Another likely threat is posed by introduced fish, such as trout (for anglers) that compete with the dippers for prey.

Conservation aims to improve the quality of the habitat through river-management policies, raise public awareness of the problems caused by use of the surrounding land, and develop an area of the planned national park in the Nevados del Aconquija, Argentina. Such measures will protect part of the dipper's range.

The rufous-throated dipper *is the rarest of the five dipper species. Dippers are the only passerines (perching birds) that are truly aquatic, living only on and around streams and rivers.*

Dodo

Raphus cucullatus

The dodo was first discovered on a remote island in the Indian Ocean in about 1507. Few people ever saw it alive, but it has since become world famous as a symbol of extinction.

The dodo is a kind of giant ground pigeon that somehow reached the island of Mauritius long ago and developed into a unique, flightless bird. The island had no native mammals and no human inhabitants, so flight was unnecessary to escape enemies. The birds could nest on the ground and roam around without risk.

Portuguese navigators discovered the dodo on Mauritius in about 1507. It was described as being unintelligent (the name possibly comes from the Portuguese *doudo*, meaning "stupid") and easy to catch and kill. The sailors would stock up with fresh meat in the form of dodos before continuing their travels. A later Dutch expedition fed their entire crew on four dodos with some to spare, but noted that the dead birds needed to be boiled for a long time before they were tender enough to eat.

Island Colonization

Subsequent visits by French and British ships led to colonization of the island. The settlers cleared the forests to make way for sugarcane. They imported pigs, monkeys, cats, and dogs; with them also came rats. The introduced animals were highly effective scavengers and predators. Although the adult dodos were large enough to defend themselves, their eggs—laid on the ground—could be swiftly gobbled up by the first pig or monkey that spotted them. The fruit trees that provided a vital part of the bird's diet vanished, and within about 155 years of its discovery the dodo was extinct.

Dead as a Dodo

No dodos were found during a visit to Mauritius in 1682. The dodo has since become an international symbol for extinction and a reminder of the pressures facing wildlife in the modern world. The expression "dead as a dodo" has even entered our language to describe something that is dead or defunct.

Our impression of what a dodo looks like may be based on drawings of the bird done long ago. The pictures make the bird look very plump. In fact, analysis of the dodo's skeletal structure suggests that it was actually a slimmer bird, more like a modern wild

COMOROS
MADAGASCAR
MAURITIUS Rodrigues
Réunion (France) former range

DATA PANEL

Dodo

Raphus cucullatus

Family: Raphidae

World population: 0 (Extinct)

Distribution: Mauritius, Indian Ocean

Habitat: Lowland forests

Size: Length: about 30 in (75 cm). Weight: up to 50 lb (23 kg)

Form: Gray, turkey-sized bird, often depicted as plump. Large, fleshy feet; tuft of tail feathers; thick, long bill measuring 9 in (20 cm) with hooked tip

Diet: Large fruit gathered from forest floor, perhaps supplemented by invertebrates, including snails and worms

Breeding: Said to lay single white egg

Related endangered species: Probably Rodrigues solitaire *(Pezophaps solitaria)* EX

Status: IUCN EX; not listed by CITES

See also: Island Biogeography **1:** 30; Introductions **1:** 54; Cassowary, Southern **3:** 28

turkey. It is possible, however, that the plumpness shown in the pictures was real. It was thought that the dodos ate large quantities of fruit in season and stored the fat in their bodies. On occasion they were said to have reached a weight of 50 pounds (23 kg).

Dodo Remains

Unusually for a forest bird, a number of bones exist for study. Some dodos appear to have fallen into rock crevices or were trapped in small caves in the volcanic lava of Mauritius, leaving their bones for scientists to discover centuries later. However, most of the bones in the world's museums come from a swamp where the modern international airport now lies. Many dodos seem to have drowned here, and collectors used to employ local people to wade around in the mud feeling for dodo bones with their bare feet.

There are no dodo skins in existence, just the head and foot of a specimen that had been kept alive in Europe. The body parts were stuffed after the bird died, but were attacked and partly defaced by insects.

The remains were rescued and are now on display in the University Museum in Oxford, England. Some museums exhibit life-sized models of the dodo, created using goose and chicken feathers.

There were stories of another species of dodo—the white dodo—living on the island of Réunion. The island is situated about 120 miles (200 km) west of Mauritius. Being flightless, it is difficult to imagine that the Mauritian dodo could have colonized Réunion. In fact, the evidence for the existence of white dodos relies on old eyewitness accounts, which may well be inaccurate. Either the sailors were mistaken about which island they saw the dodo on, or they confused the bird with a flightless ibis that lived on Réunion and is now also extinct.

The dodo *was extinct by 1682. It was probably not as plump as it was depicted in illustrations.*

Dog, African Wild

Lycaon pictus

Competition from other predators such as lions and hyenas has always been a problem for the African wild dog. Contact with people has added to the dangers, and the animal is now extinct in several countries.

Wild dogs once roamed all across the plains of Africa, but today they are rarer than the rhinoceros and in severe decline. One of the reasons is that, like other predators, the wild dog is persecuted in defense of domestic stock. The dogs' method of killing their prey—chasing in packs, then overpowering their victim and tearing it to pieces—contributes to the their reputation for being savage killers that are best eliminated. Ever since the arrival of European colonizers, wild dogs have been speared, snared, poisoned, and shot.

Contact with rapidly increasing numbers of people and domestic dogs has also created a serious danger from fatal diseases such as rabies, anthrax, and canine distemper. Many wild dogs are killed on the roads, even in protected areas like South Africa's Kruger National Park, where 24 percent of the wild dog population has been killed by road traffic.

Of all the African carnivores, this species has declined the fastest and is now regarded as endangered wherever it occurs. It is already extinct in over 60 percent of the countries that previously supported populations, including the Congo, Eritrea, Uganda, and most of West Africa

Competition

Even without man-made dangers, the wild dog is a poor survivor. It suffers severely from competition with other predators, particularly lions and hyenas. The dogs are relatively small and weak and frequently fail to prevent other predators from stealing their catch. Lions and hyenas often live at higher densities too. In the Selous Game Reserve, South Africa, for example, there are 11 lions and 32 hyenas per 40 square miles (100 sq. km), but only four wild dogs. Heavily outnumbered, the dogs are also at risk from being killed by lions.

Wild dogs hunt inefficiently. The whole pack chases a single antelope at 30 miles per hour (50 km/h) for up to

DATA PANEL

African wild dog (painted hunting dog)

Lycaon pictus

Family: Canidae

World population: Fewer than 3,000

Distribution: Formerly widespread in nonforested and nondesert areas of sub-Saharan Africa; now only in southern and eastern Africa

Habitat: From semidesert to Alpine; savanna and woodland probably preferred

Size: Length: 30–42 in (76–112 cm); height at shoulder: 30 in (75 cm). Weight: 36–80 lb (18–36 kg)

Form: A large dog with blotchy yellow, black, and white patches and a long, white-tufted tail. Each individual dog has its own special pattern, but the muzzle is always black

Diet: Mammals: mostly small antelopes

Breeding: Only the dominant pair in a pack actually breed. Up to 20 pups in a litter (usually fewer than 10) born May–July. Life span up to about 10 years

Related endangered species: Most species of wolf (*Canis* spp.)

Status: IUCN EN; not listed by CITES

See also: Populations 1: 20; Disease 1: 55; Dhole 4: 16; Dog, Bush 4: 24; Hyena, Spotted 5: 68; Wolf, Ethiopian 10: 64

3 miles (5 km). This takes a lot of energy, and the dogs need their food to recoup this cost and to raise their many offspring. If, as is too often the case, their catch is stolen by hyenas, they have to hunt again—using up still more energy. Even if hyenas stole only a quarter of the dogs' food, they would need to hunt for an impossible 12 hours a day to compensate. The dogs only thrive in areas where lions and hyenas are scarce, but such areas also tend to have fewer animals on which they can prey.

In the whole of Africa fewer than 10 wild dog populations exceed 100 animals, and there are only

The African wild dog *is now one of the rarest and most seriously threatened mammals in Africa.*

750 wild dogs left in Zimbabwe, one of the strongholds of the species. The remaining African wild dog population is split into small, widely spaced groups that are unlikely ever to meet in order to breed. If and when any of these groups also becomes extinct, there is no prospect of their being replaced by natural colonization, because dispersal over long distances through hostile farming areas and urban lands is simply not possible these days.

Dog, Bush

Speothos venaticus

Most people have never heard of the bush dog—an otterlike dog with webbed feet and a bushy tail. Sadly, this rare and curious animal is a victim of indifference and the relentless destruction of its habitat: the wet forests and grasslands of South America.

With its short legs and webbed feet, the rare bush dog of South America looks more like a short-tailed, long-legged otter than a conventional dog. Like the otter, it spends much of its time in or close to water, where it catches most of its food. However, the bush dog's prey is made up not of fish, but mainly of terrestrial or semiaquatic mammals—mostly rodents such as agoutis or pacas. By hunting as a pack and driving victims into the water, bush dogs also manage to tackle much larger animals, including capybaras (the largest rodent in the world) and rheas—large, flightless birds that can weigh almost 10 times as much as a single bush dog.

Local people's attitudes toward the bush dog vary. In some parts of their range young bush dogs are taken from the wild and kept as pets; elsewhere they are regarded as predators and are hunted and shot indiscriminately. For the most part, however, the bush dog is simply ignored.

Slash and Burn

The humid forests and damp waterside grasslands where the bush dog lives are not at risk from natural fires. The vegetation is simply too wet to burn easily, and rivers and pools tend to act as natural fire breaks. It is little wonder, therefore, that bush dogs and other water-loving animals and plants are not adapted to cope with the fires that are deliberately started and sustained to clear the land for farming. "Slash-and-burn" agricultural practices probably kill scores of bush dogs at a time and leave the survivors no home to return to once the fire has burned out.

In theory, bush dogs are protected because of their Vulnerable status. They are listed on Appendix I of CITES, so it is illegal to trade in bush dogs alive or dead. However, while forests and grasslands continue to be felled, burned, plowed, or turned over to grazing, the future of the species is in question. Regenerating forests full of young, vigorous trees are of limited use to bush dogs, since the animals need hollowed out trunks of ancient trees as dens in which to hide by night and as places to rear their young. They may also

---

DATA PANEL

Bush dog

Speothos venaticus

Family: Canidae

World population: Unknown; probably low thousands

Distribution: Parts of Panama, Colombia, Ecuador, Venezuela, The Guianas, Brazil, eastern Peru, eastern Bolivia, Paraguay, and northern Argentina

Habitat: Forest and wet grassland close to water

Size: Length head/body: 22–29.5 in (57–75 cm); tail: 4.5–6 in (12–15 cm); height at shoulder: 12 in (30 cm). Weight: 11–15.5 lb (5–7 kg)

Form: Short-legged, otterlike dog with broad head, small ears, short, bushy tail, and webbed feet; fur rich reddish brown, darkest at rear, with variable pale patch under chin

Diet: Rodents and other mammals up to and including size of capybara; birds, including rheas

Breeding: Between 1 and 6 (usually 3 or 4) pups born in rainy season after 17-week gestation; weaned at 4–5 months; mature at 10 months. May live up to 13 years in captivity; less in the wild

Related endangered species: No close relatives, but other threatened members of the dog family Canidae include red wolf (*Canis rufus*)* CR; Ethiopian wolf (*C. simensis*)* CR; African wild dog (*Lycaon pictus*)* EN; dhole (*Cuon alpinus*)* VU, and maned wolf (*Chrysocyon brachyurus*)* LRnt

Status: IUCN VU; CITES I

See also: Biomes **1:** 18; The Role of Zoos **1:** 86; Dhole **4:** 16; Wolf, Maned **10:** 70

use burrows abandoned by other animals, but such animals are also driven out by land clearance.

Conservation

There are areas of protected bush-dog habitat in national parks and wildlife reserves in South America, but even here the species is rare. Top predators, even small ones like bush dogs, never become very common because they need a lot of prey.

Bush dogs also have to share their food resources with other carnivores, some of which—like the maned wolf and the jaguar—are even more at risk. Conservation measures that favor one species must be carefully considered in case they have an adverse effect on another. The only way to help all the animals in an area is to preserve as many large areas of diverse habitat as possible.

One positive factor in an otherwise familiar story of habitat loss and declining populations is that bush dogs seem to take easily to captivity. Between 100 and 200 animals currently live in about 30 zoos and research institutes around the world, with the largest group in the Itaipu Flora and Fauna Museum in Paraguay. Much of what is known about bush dogs stems from studies of the Itaipu colony, in which the animals have bred so readily that males and females now have to be kept apart in order to prevent a population explosion and overcrowding.

The bush dog *is equally at home on land and in water. It hunts in packs by day and spends the night holed up in a burrow or hollow tree with its family.*

Dolphin, Amazon River

Inia geoffrensis

The world's largest river and its tributaries are home to the boto, or Amazon river dolphin. Pollution, dam-building, and overfishing are all threatening the future of this animal.

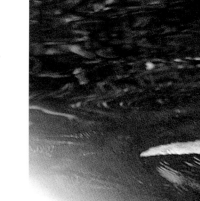

The Amazon river dolphin's range is naturally broken up into three main stretches of water, separated by extensive or perilous rapids. For this reason some scientists think that there are three distinct subspecies living in the Orinoco River in Venezuela, the Madeira River in Bolivia, and the Brazilian Amazon. However, other biologists maintain that these populations are not as separate as they seem. Every year the rivers flood, allowing large fish—and maybe also some river dolphins—to swim over and around the rapids. When the waters subside again, the dolphins become trapped, at least until the rains the following year. This phenomenon repeats itself on a smaller scale throughout the dolphin's range, with animals moving through submerged areas of forest during the flood period and sometimes getting stranded in small lakes for the duration of the dry season.

The Risks of Isolation

The cyclic ebb and flow of flood waters is fairly commonplace in the region, and the dolphins usually manage to survive a season or two in quite small lakes, as long as there are plenty of fish trapped along with them. Problems can arise, however, when the lakes are drained to irrigate crops, or if humans compete for the same fish prey as the dolphins. Once the fish in a lake are gone, no more can arrive to replace them until the forest becomes flooded again the following year.

While local activities such as fishing and irrigation threaten isolated groups of dolphins, the building of dams for hydroelectric power and flood control can damage whole populations. Dams create permanent barriers to the dolphins' passage, cutting off whole populations. These isolated groups can become inbred and vulnerable to disease and local disasters from which there is no escape either up- or downstream.

River dolphins are not normally hunted, largely because local legend has it that they harbor the souls of drowned people. The dolphins themselves are frequent victims of

DATA PANEL

Amazon river dolphin (boto, pink dolphin)

Inia geoffrensis

Family: Iniidae

World population: Unknown

Distribution: Orinoco and Amazon river systems, South America

Habitat: Rivers and flooded forest

Size: Length 5.6–10 ft (1.7–3 m). Weight: up to 350 lb (160 kg); males can be almost twice as heavy as females

Form: Large, bluish-gray to pink dolphin with long dorsal (back) ridge and large fins and tail flukes; small eyes, long snout with peglike teeth, and bulging cheeks and forehead

Diet: Mostly fish; some crustaceans and turtles

Breeding: Single calf born May–September after gestation of 10–11 months; weaned at 1 year or more; maturity depends on size rather than age. Life span 30 years or more

Related endangered species: Yangtze river dolphin (*Lipotes vexillifer*)* CR; Ganges river dolphin (*Platanista gangetica*) EN; Indus river dolphin (*P. minor*) EN

Status: IUCN VU; CITES II

See also: Drainage and Irrigation **1:** 40; Pollution **1:** 50; Dolphin, Yangtse River **4:** 28; Porpoise, Harbor **7:** 86

accidental drowning after becoming caught up in the huge nets set by local fishermen to take river fish. When this happens, the fishermen are happy enough to make use of the unplanned extra catch by using oil extracted from the dolphins' bodies as a lubricant and lamp fuel.

Contamination by Mercury

Like other top Amazon predators, including giant otters, river dolphins often suffer from the effects of mercury poisoning. Mercury is used to refine the gold that is mined in the region, and as many as 340 tons (300 tonnes) are released into the river every year. There is also a certain amount of natural mercury present in the soil, and deforestation is increasing the rate at which it is washed into the river by rainfall. Mercury combines with other chemicals to produce a compound called methyl mercury, significant quantities of which then build up in the bodies of river fish. Any animal that eats a lot of contaminated fish ends up

Amazon river dolphins *have pink skin that contains a little dark pigment. After prolonged activity the pink color becomes more pronounced as blood rushes to the surface to help the animal cool down.*

ingesting enough methyl mercury to cause serious damage, including birth deformities, muscle-wasting, nerve damage, and failure of the immune system. In humans the condition is known as Minimata disease, after the port in Japan where it was first diagnosed when a factory polluted the local water with mercury. The problem is even more severe for river dolphins, since everything they eat comes from the river.

27

EX
EW
CR
EN
VU
LR
O

Dolphin, Yangtze River

Lipotes vexillifer

Also known as the baiji, the Yangtze river dolphin is the rarest and most endangered species of whale, occupying one of the most polluted and overfished stretches of water in the world. Many biologists believe that extinction is just around the corner for this threatened dolphin.

The river dolphins are small, mainly freshwater dolphins that are found in Asia and South America. They have a long, slender snout, small eyes, and reduced vision.

The Yangtze river dolphin lives in one of the most polluted and overfished stretches of water in the world. In 1950 there were probably over 6,000 dolphins in the Yangtze River. By 1984 there were just 400, and today few estimates exceed 100. This decline has happened despite a good understanding of the causes and many national and international proposals to help stabilize the population. Sadly, most of them have come to nothing.

Only one Yangtze river dolphin—a male known as Qiqi, or Chee-chee—has been kept in captivity for any length of time. The hope was that one day a mate for Qiqi would be found. That day came in December 1995, when a large female was captured and brought to a seminatural reserve at Shishou. Qiqi was by that time rather old and suffering from diabetes and liver disease, but there were hopes that he would nonetheless father the world's first captive-bred baiji. These ambitions were dashed when the female died before the two could be introduced. Even though she was kept under close observation in the controlled conditions of the reserve, she lost condition quickly and took to swimming around its edges, perhaps in order to escape competition from a school of black finless porpoises that also lived there. While doing so one day, she became entangled in a fishing net and drowned. If, as several reports had recommended, the porpoises had been removed, the story might have had a different ending. Yet even if she had survived to bear offspring, a single breeding pair of baijis would hardly have provided an adequate basis for a captive population.

However sad, the death of this particular individual was not unusual. Nets and devices known as "rolling hooks" used to catch bottom-dwelling fish are largely responsible for the decline of the river dolphin. Dolphins need to breathe air; so, if they become trapped underwater, they drown. Many die this way. In addition, there are many deaths due to collisions with motor boats, and all in all

DATA PANEL

Yangtze river dolphin (Chinese river dolphin, baiji, whitefin dolphin)

Lipotes vexillifer

Family: Lipotidae

World population: Fewer than 200

Distribution: Yangtze (Chang Jiang) and Quiantang Rivers, China

Habitat: Fresh and brackish (slightly salty) river water, lakes, and estuaries; favors shallow water for feeding

Size: Length: 4.6–8.3 ft (1.4–2.5 m); male smaller than female. Weight: 90–365 lb (42–167 kg)

Form: Pale, bluish-gray dolphin with white underside and low, triangular dorsal (back) fin; snout long and narrow, slightly upcurved; eyes tiny, teeth small and peglike

Diet: Bottom-dwelling fish, especially catfish

Breeding: Single calf born February–May after gestation of 10–11 months; mature at 8 years. Life span up to 24 years

Related endangered species: Ganges river dolphin (*Platanista gangetica*) EN; Indus river dolphin (*P. minor*) EN; Amazon river dolphin (*Inia geoffrensis*)* VU

Status: IUCN CR; CITES I

CHINA

Yangtze

L Dongting   L Poyang

TAIWAN

VIETNAM

See also: Pollution 1: 50; Money Problems 1: 88; Dolphin, Amazon River 4: 26; Porpoise, Harbor 7: 86

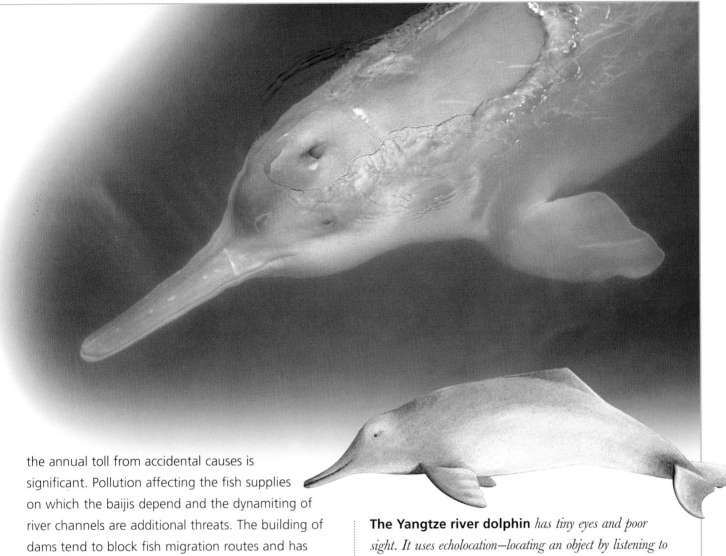

the annual toll from accidental causes is significant. Pollution affecting the fish supplies on which the baijis depend and the dynamiting of river channels are additional threats. The building of dams tend to block fish migration routes and has dramatically reduced the dolphins' prey along long stretches of the river, even affecting the few reserves where the animals are protected. Overall, the picture looks increasingly bleak.

The Yangtze river dolphin *has tiny eyes and poor sight. It uses echolocation—locating an object by listening to an echo returning from it—to find food in the muddy water.*

Saving the Baiji

There is little doubt about what needs to be done to save the baiji. Laws forbidding hunting must be enforced throughout the species' range, and the use of rolling hooks—already illegal—must also be stopped. As many dolphins as possible must be moved to reserves where they do not compete with human fisheries for their prey, and where water quality can be monitored and kept as high as possible. Such measures should in theory be easy enough to implement. In practice, because of the vast patchwork of provinces that make up modern China, national

legislation is often slow to be enforced. In many areas local social and economic factors can mean that the rules are misinterpreted or simply not applied at all.

Despite all the difficulties, there is a ray of hope on the horizon. The long-running project to build the world's biggest dam and hydroelectric power station at the Three Gorges on the Yangtze River is an example of the kind of cooperation and organization that can be achieved in this vast country. With international financial backing and scientific support and (most importantly) with the necessary political will, it may still be possible to divert some of the massive resources the project can command to the relatively small task of saving the baiji. Short of this, the world's rarest dolphin is probably doomed.

Dormouse, Common

Muscardinus avellanarius

The common dormouse is becoming less common. An arboreal (tree-dwelling) animal with very specific requirements, it has been badly affected by habitat change.

Although widespread in Europe, the common dormouse has disappeared from about half of its former range in Britain, representing a major loss in numbers and distribution. The threats facing the dormouse in Britain may also be responsible for declines in other parts of Europe.

Common dormice are arboreal; they spend almost all of their time in trees and shrubs and hardly ever come to the ground, except to hibernate. Such a lifestyle is a good defense against predators such as owls. However, it also means that the dormice have to satisfy all their food requirements up in the branches.

Hazel Haven

Dormice rely on hazelnuts, which help fatten them up in the fall in preparation for the long months of hibernation; they may stay dormant from September to April. In the past hazel trees were coppiced (grown in thickets or dense groups of small trees rather than from seed and cut back every few years to promote growth of vigorous new shoots) to provide sticks, poles, and wood for fuel. Coppicing provides ideal conditions for dormice, and they were found hibernating in hazel stumps when foresters cut back the hazel in winter to collect poles. However, demand for wood fuel decreased during the 20th century. Larger (timber) trees were encouraged and they shaded out the hazels, thereby wiping out the dormouse habitat.

A Varied Diet

Hazels and other nuts only ripen in late summer; dormice need different foods until then. They eat pollen; but since one species of flower will die away after a week or two, it is necessary for the dormice to move on to another species. The dormouse therefore needs woods with a large variety of shrubs and trees in order to ensure a continuous supply of food high up in the branches throughout the summer. Dormice also eat aphids and caterpillars, especially before fruit and nuts

Common dormouse (hazel dormouse)		Related
Muscardinus avellanarius	(15–30 g); up to 1.5 oz (43 g) just before hibernation	**endangered species:** Garden dormouse *(Eliomys quercinus)** VU; desert dormouse *(E. melanurus)* LRnt; Japanese dormouse *(Glirulus japonicus)** EN; forest dormouse *(Dryomys nitedula)* LRnt; edible dormouse *(Glis glis)* LRnt
Family: Gliridae	**Form:** Golden-yellow colored mouse with bulging black eyes and thick, bushy tail	
World population: At least 2 million		
Distribution: Western and central Europe	**Diet:** Pollen, nectar, and insects; fattens for hibernation on fruit and nuts in late summer and early fall	
Habitat: Shrub layer of deciduous woodland, hedges, and scrub		**Status:** IUCN LRnt; not listed by CITES
Size: Length head/body: 2.4–3.5 in (6–9 cm); tail: 2.2–3.2 in (5.5–8 cm). Weight: 0.5–1 oz	**Breeding:** Usually 4–5 per litter; can produce 2 or 3 litters per year, but unlikely to raise them all successfully. Life span at least 5 years in wild	

See also: Habitat Loss **1:** 38; Reintroduction **1:** 92; Dormouse, Japanese **4:** 34

The common dormouse *is a tiny, nocturnal, squirrel-like rodent that feeds mainly on fruit, nuts, and insects gathered from high up in the trees.*

become ripe. The ancient woodlands that provide all this variety have been drastically reduced, especially in Britain.

No Guarantees

Dormice live at low population densities; they are naturally scarce. As a result, small patches of woodland are simply not large enough to protect a viable population. Woods of less than about 50 acres (20 ha) may have fewer than 50 dormice present, half of them males. This is probably not enough to guarantee survival in the long term, since dormice tend to have good and bad breeding years. If the weather is bad two or three years in a row, the small populations simply die out.

Fragmentation of woodlands, through building roads or extending farmland, for example, breaks up large populations into small, vulnerable groups. If they die out, the woods are unlikely to be recolonized because dormice are reluctant to cross open ground.

Since dormice hibernate in special nests on the ground, they are also at risk from being eaten by foraging pigs or trampled on by wandering cattle. Such incidents have probably wiped out small populations in the past. Over most of the dormouse's habitat in Europe the threats are gradually increasing, but in Britain the situation is already very serious.

During the 1990s reintroductions of captive-bred animals were carried out in Britain to restore dormice to areas from which they had disappeared. They have been successful, although the released dormice need support in the form of nest boxes and extra food for the first few weeks.

Dormouse, Garden

Eliomys quercinus

The garden dormouse can be locally abundant, but the species as a whole is in decline in many parts of Europe. No one really knows the reasons why.

The garden dormouse is one of about 20 species in 10 genera in its family. Its bold, black "mask" (a stripe on each side of its face) gives it the look of a bandit. It is widespread in Continental Europe, where it is a familiar sight on farms and in villages. It also comes into people's houses, so it is often seen and identified.

Ground-Dwelling Lifestyle

Most dormice live in trees, but garden dormice spend much of their time on the ground, living in burrows or among rocks. They may also make nests in crevices of buildings or in abandoned birds' nests. Like other dormice, they are excellent climbers, even managing to scale relatively smooth surfaces. Despite their agility, garden dormice do not travel far and rarely venture more than 200 yards (150 m) from their nest.

Garden dormice live mainly in deciduous or coniferous woodland, but they are also found in gardens, vineyards, sand dunes, and on bare rocky screes high in the mountains. This suggests that they can survive in a variety of conditions by eating a range of different foods. The dormouse's diet ranges from acorns to bird eggs and beetles. Its narrow snout enables it to poke under stones and logs to seek out insect larvae and hidden seeds.

In winter garden dormice hibernate, a factor that aids their survival in cold countries such as Finland and at high altitudes in Bavaria, Germany, where the ground is covered with snow, and food is hard to find.

Mysterious Decline

The garden dormouse is a very flexible and adaptable species and can be locally abundant, with up to 20 animals per acre (50 per ha). However, the species has been getting scarcer throughout the 20th century. It is now extinct in Croatia and parts of Slovakia, and is rare across eastern Europe in Lithuania, Latvia, the Czech Republic, and eastern Germany. Along with other dormouse species the garden dormouse is legally protected by the Berne Convention and the laws of individual European countries.

In Corsica the garden dormouse is said to be suffering from competition with brown rats. However, rats are normally rare or

DATA PANEL

Garden dormouse

Eliomys quercinus

Family: Gliridae

World population: Unknown, but in the thousands

Distribution: Europe south to the Mediterranean and North Africa, north to Finland, and east to Russia

Habitat: Mainly woodland; also dry habitats, including vineyards and mountains up to 6,560 ft (2,000 m)

Size: Length head/body: 4–6.5 in (10–17 cm); tail: 3.5–6 in (9–15 cm). Weight: 1.6–4.2 oz (45–120 g). Weight increases before hibernation to 7.4 oz (210 g)

Form: Reddish brown or gray rodent with black stripe on each side of its face; large ears; white belly and paws; long, furry tail with white, flattened tuft at the end

Diet: Buds, nuts, fruit, insects, eggs; occasionally baby mice and birds

Breeding: One or 2 litters of 4–6 (up to 9) young born per year after 4-week gestation. Life span can exceed 5 years

Related endangered species: Black-tailed dormouse *(Eliomys melanurus)* LRnt; Japanese dormouse *(Glirulus japonicus)** EN; Chinese forest dormouse *(Dryomys sichuanensis)* EN

Status: IUCN VU; not listed by CITES

See also: Natural Extinction 1: 34; Dormouse, Common 4: 30; Dormouse, Japanese 4: 34; Souslik, European 9: 18

absent in the forests and rocky mountainsides where many garden dormice live, so competition with rats cannot be the only explanation for its disappearance over such a wide range of different habitats and in so many countries.

Humans pose no direct threat. Unlike the edible dormouse—the largest of the dormice (also known as the fat dormouse and considered a delicacy in Roman times, when they were specially reared for food)—the garden dormouse has never been hunted; nor is its skin of value. Animal predators such as owls do not represent a substantial threat and are certainly unable to exterminate whole populations. All dormice have an

The garden dormouse *has distinctive black markings around the eyes. A nocturnal animal, it lives in small social groups on the ground and in trees and bushes. Dormice hibernate and have a reputation as sleepy animals. The edible and common dormice stay dormant for longest: from September to April.*

interesting adaptation to evade capture. If a predator grabs at the tail, the thin skin slips off, allowing the dormouse to escape. The tail later drops off, but the dormouse survives. As yet no one knows why, despite such adaptability and resilience, the garden dormouse is in decline, or what can be done about it.

Dormouse, Japanese

Glirulus japonicus

The Japanese dormouse, or yamane, is rare and poorly known, not least because it lives in an inaccessible habitat and is active only at night. However, people's awareness of this tiny creature has increased as a result of publicity.

Like the hazel dormouse of Europe, the Japanese dormouse is small, nocturnal, and lives in dense undergrowth and among the tops of trees. It is therefore almost impossible to see in the wild. Moreover, its forest home is on steep mountain slopes, where it is very difficult for humans to move around, even in daylight. Steep terrain is no problem for the incredibly agile Japanese dormouse. It scurries around at high speed and hangs upside down from branches and twigs, searching the leaves and bark for insects, which it devours eagerly. The dormouse eats caterpillars, aphids, small beetles, and moths.

In season the Japanese dormouse will travel along the branches to find flowers from which it can take nectar and pollen. Later in the summer it gorges itself on seeds and berries such as those of the akebia vine, all of which it collects among the branches of trees rather than from the ground. The animal feeds in preparation for winter, accumulating large amounts of fat that will support its slowed-down metabolism for at least five months of hibernation. Like the hazel dormouse, it will weave a summer nest consisting of a round ball among the branches, using moss, lichen, and bark collected from the trees as the main building material. It also nests in hollow trees and crevices.

In winter the dormouse seeks out sheltered places that are cool but do not suffer from frosts. Thick, hollow trees are suitable, but the dormouse may hibernate below ground, and those dormice that live higher up the mountains where it is colder sometimes come into buildings.

Living at high altitudes, occasionally up to nearly 9,000 feet (2,900 m) above sea level, the Japanese dormouse experiences summers that are cool, short, and rather wet. Some years are worse than others,

DATA PANEL

Japanese dormouse (yamane)

Glirulus japonicus

Family: Gliridae

World population: Unknown, but said to be small and declining

Distribution: Japanese islands of Honshu, Kyushu, and Shikoka

Habitat: Mountain forests, generally 1,250–5,500 ft (400–1,800 m) above sea level

Size: Length head/body: 2.5–3.2 in (6.5–8 cm); tail: 1.6–2.2 in (4–5.5 cm). Weight: 0.5–1.4 oz (14–40 g)

Form: Pale olive or gray-brown mouse with dark stripe down middle of the back. Dense, soft fur; tail flattened and fluffy

Diet: Fruit, flowers, insects, and occasional bird eggs

Breeding: Up to 7 young (usually 4), born June–July or later; 1 or 2 litters per year. Life span unknown, but may be about 5 years

Related endangered species: Chinese dormouse (*Dryomys sichuanensis*) EN; common dormouse (*Muscardinus avellanarius*)* LRnt; Iranian dormouse (*Myomimus setzeri*) EN; mouse-tailed dormice (*M. roachi* and *M. personatus*) VU; garden dormouse (*Eliomys quercinus*)* VU; African dormouse (*Graphiurus ocularis*) VU

Status: IUCN EN; not listed by CITES

See also: Education 1: 94; Dormouse, Common 4: 30; Dormouse, Garden 4: 32

and bad weather must contribute to the scarcity of the species. Reproductive rates are low anyway, with females usually producing only about four young per year. Some females may have second litters, but breeding late allows insufficient time for the babies to become fat enough to survive hibernation during the winter. Breeding success is lower still in years when the weather is bad, or when there is little food.

Decline

The Japanese dormouse appears to be in decline, and as much as half its population may have been lost in the last 10 years or so. The threats are mainly from habitat loss and fragmentation of remaining forests into patches that are too small to support populations.

Forest clearance remains a threat to the Japanese dormouse, and the species has been classified by the IUCN as Endangered. However, the animal is so difficult to study and so poorly known that it is possible that it is actually more abundant than people realize. Being better known and appreciated by people is the species' best defense for the future.

Going Public

There have been recent campaigns to educate people about the Japanese dormouse. The animals have been shown on Japanese television, and yamane merchandise, such as T-shirts, has been produced. More people are becoming aware of the animals and taking an interest in their conservation. The Japanese government has even designated the dormouse a national symbol. A yamane museum has opened where visiting schoolchildren can watch the dormice feeding at night in the trees outside.

Where small areas of woodland have been isolated by the building of roads and rail tracks, efforts have been made to create bridges to assist the dormice in crossing the open gaps created, thereby allowing them to gain access to feeding trees that might otherwise be difficult to reach. It also helps prevent the small remnant populations from becoming isolated and inbred. This process reduces the genetic variation within the population and so makes the animals more susceptible to weakness and premature death.

The Japanese dormouse, or yamane, is rare, but recent publicity and educational campaigns in Japan have succeeded in making it a widely appreciated national treasure.

Dragon Fish

Scleropages formosus

A fishing eagle hunting over the forests of central Sumatra spotted a large fish in the foaming waters of a stream below. It swooped from the skies, dived into the water, and mated with the armor-plated fish. Thus the dragon fish was born.

So went the legend of the dragon fish. As is often the case, the story is a somewhat fanciful but not unreasonable explanation of the facts. The remarkable union between a fish and a bird seemed plausible given the large yolks to which baby dragon fish are attached during the first weeks of their development when they incubate inside their father's mouth. Dragon fish eggs have a spherical yolk that can measure up to 0.7 inches (1.8 cm) in diameter, making them larger than those of many bird species.

It is likely that the legend of the dragon fish was also reinforced by observations. People may have seen predatory birds attempting to prey on dragon fish, although the fish's thick, immensely strong scales probably protected it from such aerial attacks. If a fishing eagle or other bird of prey were to dive onto a dragon fish, causing a great deal of splashing and foaming in the process, the chances are that it would leave empty-handed (or empty-taloned). It is easy to see how a failed attack (or more likely many failed attacks observed over time) could have been interpreted as mating rather than hunting.

A Fish of Many Forms

Dragon fish are found in eastern Asia, including Malaysia, the Philippines, Vietnam, and Indonesia. Doubt exists about the Myanmar (Burma) populations, and the species may now be extinct in Thailand. The fish are known variously as the Asian arowana, Asian bonytongue, Malayan bonytongue, and emperor fish. In their native waters three names are regularly used: *cherek kelesa*, *ikan arowana* (in Malaysia), and *Lóng Yú* (in Chinese-speaking countries).

The dragon fish occurs in three color forms in the wild (with regional modifications):

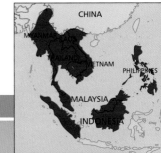

DATA PANEL		
Dragon fish *Scleropages formosus* **Family:** Osteoglossidae **World population:** Unknown **Distribution:** Cambodia, Malaysia, Philippines, Vietnam, Indonesia (Kalimantan and Sumatra). Possibly Myanmar (Burma); may now be extinct in Thailand **Habitat:** Still or slow-flowing waters that may be turbid (muddy) or heavily vegetated	**Size:** Length: up to 35 in (90 cm); usually much smaller **Form:** Torpedo-shaped body with pointed head, large eyes, and large mouth with barbels (whiskers). Thick, strong scales. Three color forms: green/silver, gold, and red **Diet:** A wide range of invertebrates and small vertebrates may be eaten. They are usually taken from the surface or upper part of the water column, but may occasionally also be plucked off branches above water	**Breeding:** About 30 eggs (but as many as 90 or more) are laid and are incubated orally by the male for 5–6 weeks; main breeding season July–December. Mature at 3–4 years **Related endangered species:** Spotted or southern saratoga *(Scleropages leichardti)* LRnt; pirarucu *(Arapaima gigas)** DD **Status:** IUCN EN; CITES I

See also: Exploitation of Live Animals **1:** 49; Pirarucu **7:** 76

The dragon fish, *particularly the red color form, is highly regarded throughout east Asia, where captive-breeding programs have ensured its survival.*

green/silver, gold, and red. The last of these is deemed the most valuable. Captive-bred varieties include crosses between the different color forms as well as color-selected types, such as the rainbow dragon. Occasionally, albinos have been reported.

Breeding can occur throughout the year, but is at its peak between July and December. Actual mating is preceded by a long period of courtship and bonding that can last two or three months. The females (which have a single ovary) will lay about 30 eggs—although over 90 have been reported—which, once fertilized, are picked up by the male in its mouth. From that point onward the female plays no further part in the process. The male, however, will incubate the eggs in its mouth for between five and six weeks, by which time the young fish (fry) can attain a length of nearly 3.5 inches (9 cm).

Fears for the Fish of Good Fortune

The dragon fish is held in high esteem in Asia, where it is believed to bring health, wealth, and luck to its owners. It is kept in aquaria throughout the region and is also much sought after by east Asian communities all over the world. Specialized Western aquarists are also interested in the species, but the large size that adult specimens can attain places the dragon fish outside the reach of most enthusiasts.

Fears for the continued survival of the dragon fish in the wild—probably as a result of overcollection—led to the species being listed under Appendix I of CITES in 1975. At one time the dragon fish was classified as Insufficiently Known by the IUCN, but its status has since been changed to Endangered.

Whether the concern over the fish's survival is fully justified or not remains open to debate. Populations have become established from captive-bred specimens in a government plan in Singapore. Monitored captive-breeding programs in other forms and other east Asian countries have also resulted in the establishment of registered farms that are licensed to export the species under a CITES Appendix I provision.

Dragon, Southeastern Lined Earless

Tympanocryptis lineata pinguicolla

The little-known southeastern lined earless dragon seems to be surviving against all odds. Current research is exploring its way of life in order to safeguard its future.

The discovery of the southeastern lined earless dragon on a farm near Cooma in New South Wales, Australia, came as a surprise to herpetologists (those who study reptiles and amphibians), since the area was thought to be an unsuitable environment. In spite of the land being grazed for almost 200 years, the dragon had survived there. It was previously thought to live in only three restricted locations in the Majura and Jerrabomberra valleys in the Australian Capital Territory. Once widely distributed, its range had been reduced after the native grassland was gradually destroyed by urban development, industry, and agriculture, eventually making it one of Australia's rarest reptiles.

Today only about 5 percent of Australia's native temperate grassland remains. It is a mainly treeless area with kangaroo grass, wallaby grass, and spear grass. The dragons use the open areas for basking and hunting, but the grasses also provide shade and refuge; the dragons are known to use spider burrows in the soil and are sometimes found under rocks.

As both the common and scientific names suggest (*tympanum* means the cavity in the ear), the lizard lacks the ear openings that are common to most, but not all lizards. The family Agamidae is found only in the Old World. Australia has several different genera of the family, some of which (including *Tympanocryptis* species) are known as dragons. One of the best known, and most popular with reptile hobbyists, is the bearded dragon.

Protection Proposals

In 1996 the dragon was listed as an endangered species under Australia's Nature Conservation Act. An action plan for its conservation was formed, linked to the action plan for natural temperate grassland and to plans for other species of plants and animals that occur in the grasslands. The aim was to provide for further study of the unknown aspects of the earless dragon's way of life.

Exact numbers in the wild are not yet known. Current research shows young lizards to be more numerous than adults, suggesting that adults, especially females, do not live long after breeding. A few adult females survive into their second year. Youngsters take only a few weeks to reach adult size.

DATA PANEL

Southeastern lined earless dragon

Tympanocryptis lineata pinguicolla

Family: Agamidae

World population: Unknown

Distribution: Restricted sites in Australian Capital Territory and New South Wales, Australia

Habitat: Well-drained, natural temperate grassland with open spaces and grass tussocks

Size: Length: 8.5 in (22 cm)

Form: Stout body; short limbs; tail slightly longer than body. Dark brown or grayish bands across back and tail, producing effective camouflage; 3 light stripes extend along dorsal surface. Underside can be uniform light color or similar to body. Many adults have yellow or orange on throat, sometimes on side of head, and along flanks. Pale-colored stripe extends between eyes. Dorsal surface covered with scattered, spiny scales

Diet: Insects; some plant material

Breeding: One clutch of 1–6 eggs; (average 3–4 eggs)

Related endangered species: Other members of Agamidae family, including Yinnietharra rock dragon (*Ctenophorus yinnietharra*) VU; spineless forest lizard (*Calotes liocephalus*) EN; and Tennent's leaf-nosed lizard (*Ceratophora tennentii*) EN

Status: IUCN VU; not listed by CITES

See also: Pasture 1: 38; Research 1: 84; Education 1: 94; Skink, Pygmy Blue-Tongued 9: 4

Other factors such as habitat requirements and social interaction have also yet to be determined. Research has shown that the dragons move considerable distances within their site. Captive specimens show aggressive reactions toward each other and form a hierarchy based on size and color. It is possible that even in the wild, where territory is less restricted, the same aggressive traits are displayed.

The fact that a lizard population had survived in a grazed area gave rise to hopes for the future of the species; grassland habitat is often destroyed by overgrazing to the extent that other animals are driven out. However, the dragon's relatively small range is still vulnerable to further damage and fragmentation. Plowing of land, the application of pesticides, and the effects of industry and urban development are all potential hazards. Urban expansion brings domestic pets and attracts some feral (wild) animals, giving rise to increased predation. Industry requires roads, and agriculture, irrigation projects.

New Reserves

The extent of the lined earless dragon's range is still being determined. (One dragon site has even been found inside a military firing range.) Some of the lizard's territory is in private hands; persuading landowners of the importance of the dragons and educating the public are vital. At present the species is not known to occur on any reserve, so the creation of new reserves is being considered. Although many organizations are cooperating to protect the lined earless dragon, all sites except for one in Australian Capital Territory are in areas included in development proposals for urban expansion.

Several conservation laws exist under which various protective measures could be exercised. Moving the lizards is not considered possible since there are no suitable areas outside the sites. Much dragon territory is currently used for grazing. The

survival of the dragons at Cooma may have proved that groups are able to carve out an existence in grazed areas. However, it is likely that a lack of suitable grassland would eventually have devastating effects on the species. Current plans aim to protect at least two sites to safeguard the dragon's future.

The southeastern lined earless dragon's *diet is known to consist of spiders and insects, but captive specimens will take fruit.*

Drill

Mandrillus leucophaeus

A large, short-tailed monkey and a relative of the mandrill, the drill is the highest primate conservation priority on mainland Africa. Emergency measures are needed to prevent this vulnerable species and its habitat from disappearing.

The dense, lowland forests of northern Cameroon and the island of Bioko, which lies 20 miles (34 km) off the African coast, are the last refuges of the drill—a monkey that is closely related to the mandrill. Both the drill and the mandrill are baboons. They are powerful, stocky animals that will fight if disturbed.

The drill's range is thought to be only 15,000 square miles (40,000 sq. km), with most of the remaining population living in one national park at Korup in Cameroon. This alarming situation led the IUCN to make the drill their highest priority African primate in 1995. Since then there has been a concerted effort to set aside and protect areas of habitat in order to provide the drills with some security in the future.

Drills are omnivores: They eat fruit, vegetable material, and small animals. They are forest-dwellers and prefer to live in mature, untouched forest, known as primary forest. Drills have begun to return to areas where felled trees have been allowed to regenerate, but these so-called secondary forests are by no means ideal habitats for the monkeys. They tend to have fewer species of mature trees and provide a restricted range of foods. They are not able to support whole populations of drills; but where they exist alongside existing patches of primary forest, they are better than nothing.

Unfortunately, very few felled forest areas are allowed to return to nature in this way. Occasionally, some are replanted with nonnative tree species that might make profitable timber in the future, but in the meantime they offer little to support the drills. Most of the clear-felled land is plowed over and planted with crops such as manioc, bananas, and oil palms. The drills can and do eat the crops, much to the annoyance of local farmers. The animals are therefore often treated as pests and are shot or trapped to prevent further damage to crops.

NIGERIA

CAMEROON

Bioko
(Equatorial Guinea)

EQUATORIAL GUINEA

GABON

DATA PANEL

Drill

Mandrillus leucophaeus

Family: Cercopithecidae

World population: 3,000 (1999 estimate)

Distribution: Cameroon, southeastern Nigeria, and Bioko Island (Equatorial Guinea)

Habitat: Lowland forest

Size: Length: 18–35.5 in (45–90 cm); male up to twice as big as female. Weight: about 33 lb (15 kg)

Form: Large, stout-bodied baboon with short tail. Large head with black face fringed with white fur; fur elsewhere grayish brown. Males have mane of thicker fur and hairless buttocks of varying shades of red, pink, and blue

Diet: Fruit, seeds, roots, fungi, insects, and some small vertebrates

Breeding: Single young born at any time of year, but mostly December–April after gestation of about 8 months; mature at 5 years. Life span up to 29 years

Related endangered species: Various macaques, monkeys, and apes, including the mandrill *(Mandrillus sphinx)* VU

Status: IUCN EN; CITES I

See also: Life Strategies **1:** 24; Hunting **1:** 42; Baboon, Gelada **2:** 46; Macaque, Barbary **6:** 54; Macaque, Japanese **6:** 56

Dominant Males

Drills are among the mammals that have traditionally been hunted for "bush meat," which is considered a delicacy by people in some areas of West Africa. Hunters equipped with rifles, spotlights (when hunting at night), and refrigerated trucks can make significant profits by killing large numbers of animals that they then sell in local markets.

Drills live in conspicuous groups of between 20 and 25 individuals. They cannot travel rapidly overland or through the trees, so a hunter with a rifle can kill many animals in a very short time. Often whole social groups are wiped out at once. Not only is this catastrophic in terms of lives lost, it wreaks havoc among any surviving members of the troop. When senior members of the group's hierarchy have been killed, it takes some time for a new order to be established, and the struggle for power will have its own casualties. Drill troops are dominated by an alpha male who is usually the biggest and strongest. A male that becomes

dominant by default after the old alpha male is killed may not be as effective as his predecessor at defending the troop and fathering healthy offspring. An unworthy leader will be replaced sooner or later, but the changeover only prolongs the period of upheaval and adjustment that the animals have to make. Adult female drills produce an average of only one young every two to three years; sometimes there are six years between births. Breeding success will be reduced during periods of social unrest within the troop, resulting in an even slower rate of recovery.

To secure a safer future for the drill, a protected and suitable habitat must be set aside. A conservation plan will need to include persuading and educating the local people of the need to stop hunting the drill.

The drill (right) is a little smaller than the mandrill (left) and has an all-black face with whitish hairs. The buttocks of both animals display colors of varying intensity depending on the individual's age, sex, breeding condition, social status, and mood.

Duck, Labrador

Camptorhynchus labradorius

The distinctive and attractive Labrador duck was never common and became extinct in the late 19th century. The reason for its disappearance remains a mystery.

The male Labrador duck was one of the most attractive among a colorful group of birds. It had a white head, black body, and large white wing patches. As with other species of ducks, the female was a drab brown, probably indicating that she alone was responsible for incubating their eggs. Such sexual "dimorphism" (two distinct forms) is seen in most species of duck. Dull colors are an advantage to the female, concealing her and her precious brood from the eyes of predators. The male, meanwhile, is free to exploit his fine appearance to attract other mates or to display in competition with other males.

Mysterious Birds

However, this is all guesswork based on what we know of duck species in general; we know almost nothing about the Labrador duck itself. Today it seems amazing that such a large and distinctive bird living in a well-populated part of North America should remain such a mystery. After all, it has been extinct for barely a century.

Little information is available about Labrador ducks. Records show that they used to turn up in the meat and fish markets in New York, New Jersey, and Maryland, having been shot along nearby coasts in the winter. The famous American naturalist and bird painter J. J. Audubon claimed to have seen them as far south as Chesapeake Bay, Virginia. They were also known to be winter visitors in the Bay of Fundy, between Nova Scotia and New Brunswick, and along the coast of Long Island.

The Labrador ducks' breeding areas seem to have been farther north, probably along the Gulf of St. Lawrence and coastal Labrador, and would have been frozen for many months of the year. The ducks apparently retreated south to sandy bays, sheltered inlets, harbors, and estuaries. Here the sea would not freeze, and they would be able to find food.

Despite the fact that Labrador ducks were seen regularly in markets, they were not a popular food, and it would appear that nobody made special efforts to hunt many of them. The ducks were said to be wary and difficult to shoot anyway. This is in direct contrast to many extinct and endangered bird species that were highly sought after and hunted down ruthlessly.

Death by Natural Causes

Instead, the Labrador duck seems never to have been a successful or

---

DATA PANEL

Labrador duck

Camptorhynchus labradorius

Family: Anatidae

World population: 0 (Extinct)

Distribution: Unknown; probably bred along the Gulf of St. Lawrence and coastal Labrador, Canada, and wintered from Nova Scotia to Chesapeake Bay, Virginia

Habitat: Unknown; wintered along seacoasts

Size: Length head/body: 12–15 in (30–40 cm); tail: 2 in (5 cm)

Form: Male strikingly black and white; female brown

Diet: Unknown; probably a specialized diet, perhaps soft plant material or invertebrates such as mollusks

Breeding: Unknown

Related endangered species: Chubut steamerduck (*Tachyeres leucocephalus*) LRnt

Status: IUCN EX; not listed by CITES

CANADA

UNITES STATES

probable former range

See also: Specialization 1: 28; Natural Extinction 1: 34; Duck, White-Headed 4: 44

abundant species and appears to have died out from natural causes. Perhaps there was some catastrophic event in its breeding areas, which may have been marshes or on small islands offshore. Or maybe its extinction was due to specialization.

The Labrador duck was peculiar in having an unusually large number of special plates or grooves inside its beak and soft corners to the end of the bill. Such features usually indicate a particular feeding method, one that probably relied heavily on specific foods. Perhaps the special beak was used to deal with mollusks or to sieve tiny insect larvae or shrimp from mud or water. Such a lifestyle would be risky, relying on an abundance of food and little competition for it.

A rare species will always be in danger of extinction simply because its population is small to begin with. Breeding, feeding, or habitat problems will have an immediate effect on numbers. We will never know for sure what happened to the Labrador duck, but it is not thought that the small numbers shot by hunters could in themselves have caused its extinction.

The Labrador duck *was always rare, and its habits and lifestyle are still a mystery. The male had striking black-and-white plumage, while the female was mainly brown.*

Perhaps the birds or their eggs and young were taken from their few breeding grounds by people or by an invasion of predators, reducing numbers to such low levels that hunting then finished them off completely. Populations seem to have declined gradually. The duck disappeared from the markets between 1850 and 1870. The last recorded specimen was probably the one shot in the fall of 1875 on Long Island, New York. (This is now in the Smithsonian Institution.) A less likely final record is for 1878, when one was said to have been shot near Elmira, New York. Another had been shot in 1871 on Mana Island, New Brunswick. Today there are about 50 known specimens in museums, five of them in a single glass case in the American Museum of Natural History in New York. It is one of five or six species of American birds that have become extinct in the last 200 years.

Duck, White-Headed

Oxyura leucocephala

Long-term population declines for the white-headed duck have recently intensified as a result of habitat loss at a key wintering site. Threats of competition from the introduced North American ruddy duck have also been a problem.

The white-headed duck probably had a global population of over 100,000 in the early 20th century; in the 1930s an estimated 50,000 wintered on the Caspian Sea. However, by 1991 the population was estimated at a mere 19,000 ducks. This reduction in numbers was matched by a large decline in breeding range. Over the last 100 years the white-headed duck has become extinct as a breeding bird in Albania, Azerbaijan, Corsica, Hungary, Italy, Israel, Morocco, and the former Yugoslavia. Despite the historical declines, however, there was some optimism in 1991, since the population was thought to be relatively stable.

Since 1991 that optimism has faded. Numbers appear to have plummeted over the last decade to fewer than 10,000 birds. The decline has been most severe at what was the most important wintering site, Burdur Gölü in Turkey. In 1991 about 10,900 birds wintered there, but in 1996 only 1,270 were recorded. Obviously, some of the birds have simply scattered to other wetland sites, and wintering numbers have increased elsewhere in the eastern Mediterranean region. They include the doubling of the population at Lake Vistonis, Greece, with other large increases in Bulgaria and Romania. However, the counts do not compensate for the very large declines at Burdur Gölü.

Reasons for the Decline

The large historical declines are mostly the result of extensive drainage of wetlands, particularly in the former Soviet Union and Spain. Over 50 percent of breeding habitat was destroyed during the 20th century, and the remaining sites are especially vulnerable to eutrophication (overenrichment by nutrients, particularly nitrates and phosphates) and pollution. The range of threats includes industrial, domestic, and agricultural pollution, sedimentation, and water extraction, as seen at Burdur Gölü and the Sultan marshes in central southern Turkey. At Lake Vistonis drowning in fishing nets is a severe threat. Dead birds have also been found in nets at sites in Spain and Turkey.

DATA PANEL

White-headed duck

Oxyura leucocephala

Family: Anatidae

World population: Fewer than 10,000 birds

Distribution: Algeria, Spain, and Tunisia; most birds breed in Russia and Kazakhstan, smaller populations in Afghanistan, Iran, Mongolia, Turkey, and Uzbekistan. Eastern populations occur and winter in the eastern Mediterranean, Middle East, Central Asia, and the Indian subcontinent

Habitat: Breeds on small, shallow, freshwater or brackish lakes with dense vegetation at fringes. Winter lakes are larger and deeper with little emergent vegetation. In Spain and Tunisia, artificial lagoons and reservoirs

Size: Length: 17–19 in (43–48 cm); wingspan: 24.5–27.5 in (62–70 cm). Weight: male 25–32 oz (720–900 g); female 19–28 oz (550–800 g)

Form: Chestnut-brown diving duck; long tail, often cocked vertically. Male has white head, black cap, and blue bill, swollen at base. Female has pale face with dark cap, and cheek stripe; blackish, less swollen bill

Diet: In Spain benthic (bottom-dwelling) chironomid larvae and pupae; wintering birds in Greece feed primarily on polychaete worms

Breeding: Polygamous (has more than 1 mate); nests in dense reedbeds, often on top of old coot nests. Timing is variable, with 4–9 eggs laid April and early July. Incubation takes 3–3.5 weeks, fledging 8–9 weeks

Related endangered species: Twenty-one others, including pink-headed duck (*Rhodonessa caryophyllacea*) CR

Status: IUCN EN; CITES II

See also: Pollution 1: 50; Inbreeding and Interbreeding 1: 56; Duck, Labrador 4: 42

White-headed duck *populations have suffered through widespread habitat loss and cross-breeding with the ruddy duck.*

Ruddy Duck Danger

While a major problem for the white-headed duck is habitat loss, western European populations are also threatened by hybridization and competition with the North American ruddy duck. The ruddy duck was introduced to Britain in the 1950s and is now spreading across western and into central Europe. It has been seen in 20 countries, and breeding has been recorded in six. This introduced species cross-breeds readily with the white-headed duck, and hybrids are fully fertile; second-generation birds have also been collected in Spain. The real concern is that the ruddy duck will spread eastward into the core of the white-headed duck's range. If it spreads into Algeria, Turkey, or Russia, the size of the wetlands—which are infrequently monitored—will make control impossible.

Conservation Measures

Measures are being taken to control the ruddy duck in France, Portugal, Spain, and the Netherlands. In Britain a regional control trial is assessing whether a wider, longer-term strategy is necessary and practicable. The Spanish control program is one element of a highly effective conservation strategy that was started in 1979. Since then a reduction in illegal hunting, the regeneration of natural vegetation, the release of captive-bred birds into the wild, and from 1989 shooting of ruddy ducks and hybrids has led to a dramatic population recovery.

The challenge is to replicate the success of the Spanish program for more easterly populations. The effective protection of wetlands in Russia and Kazahkstan is a high priority. Without such protection it is almost certain that the white-headed duck will continue its dramatic decline.

Dugong

Dugong dugon

The vegetarian dugong has been hunted to the brink of extinction throughout most of its range. The future of the species may now rest almost exclusively with the fate of one population living off the coast of Australia.

Sightings of dugongs and their kind are often said to have given rise to stories of mermaids. The large, blubbery animals, with their huge bristle-studded lips and tough, gray hide, may be far removed from the traditional image of the fabled sea maidens, but dugongs are nevertheless graceful, gentle, and curious animals. In areas where they are not persecuted they readily approach divers and small boats, apparently attracted by unusual sounds. Dugongs have excellent hearing and good eyesight.

The dugong's alternative name of "sea cow" is fitting, since the animal's behavior reflects that of the land cow. Like its land-dwelling namesake, it lives mostly in herds and it feeds on underwater pastures of sea grass. It has intelligence similar to a cow or deer, and its flesh is reputed to taste much like veal.

The dugong is the only living species in its family. Its closest relative, Steller's sea cow, was hunted to extinction over a period of just 27 years during the 18th century.

Hunting and Natural Hazards

At one time dugongs were common around the edges of the Indian and southwestern Pacific Oceans. However, dugongs make good eating and have other uses. They have been hunted for meat, their oil, and their thick hides, which produce good leather. Dugongs are mammals, so they have to breathe air. Consequently, when they come up from a dive to breathe at the surface, they are easy to catch and kill in nets. The dugong has now been brought to the brink of extinction across its range.

Dugongs also face a number of natural hazards. In the past, when the animals were common, the population could withstand losses from predation by sharks, killer whales, and estuarine crocodiles. It could even recover from local catastrophes, such as flooded rivers that dumped thousands of tons of silt over their sea grass pastures, causing mass starvation. Today, with so many dugong populations at the very limit of viability, such pressures could mean extinction for the remaining groups.

The plight of the African and Asian populations is cause for extreme concern. In 1998 it was reported that the last remaining viable population of East African dugongs had probably declined to just 21 individuals—barely a sustainable number. Around the coasts of Madagascar, India, Sri Lanka, and Southeast Asia the situation is equally critical. The dugong is protected by law throughout its range, but in many areas the law is difficult to enforce. Illegal killing undoubtedly still occurs, sometimes by accident, sometimes deliberately in order to obtain food, hides, and body parts for use in traditional medicines and treatments; substances derived from the dugongs are used as aphrodisiacs.

Last Stronghold

Dugongs once lived around the Australian coast in great herds numbering many thousands of individuals. Although such herds are almost certainly a thing of the past, groups of several hundred dugongs are still reported off the coast of western Australia. However, it is the seas between Australia's northern coast and

See also: Life Strategies **1:** 24; Cow, Steller's Sea **3:** 70; Manatee, Florida **6:** 68

DATA PANEL

Dugong (sea cow)

Dugong dugon

Family: Dugongidae

World population: Fewer than 150,000

Distribution: Indian and southwestern Pacific Oceans

Habitat: Shallow seas of tropical coasts

Size: Length head to tail: 8–9 ft (2.4–2.7 m), occasionally up to 13 ft (4 m). Weight: 300–800 lb (230–360 kg), occasionally up to 2,000 lb (900 kg)

Form: Large, superficially seallike mammal with gray, almost hairless hide, jointed front flippers, and broad, flat tail. Small eyes and large upper lip with tough, bristly pads

Diet: Mostly sea grasses; occasionally green and brown seaweed

Breeding: Single young (rarely twins) born every 3–7 years at any time of year, after gestation of 13–14 months. Young first graze at 3 months; fully weaned at 18 months; mature at 9–10 years. Life span up to 73 years

Related endangered species: Steller's sea cow *(Hydrodamalis gigas)** EX. No close living relatives but 3 species of manatee listed as Vulnerable: Amazon manatee *(Trichechus inunguis)*, Florida manatee *(T. manatus)*,* and African manatee *(T. senegalensis)*

Status: IUCN VU; CITES II (Australian population); elsewhere CITES I

the island of New Guinea that represent the closest thing the dugong has to a stronghold. Here a limited amount of hunting by native Australians and Torres Strait Islanders is still permitted. About 1,200 dugongs are killed in the region each year, mostly by nets or harpoons. Such hunting is strictly monitored because there are fears that even limited kills might be too much. It remains to be seen if hunting will result in the same fate for the dugong as it did for Steller's sea cow—extinction.

The dugong *uses its tail for swimming and its flippers for steering and "walking" along the seabed while it feeds. The tail has a distinctive concave trailing edge, which helps distinguish the dugong from the similar manatees.*

Duiker, Jentink's

Cephalophus jentinki

Jentink's is one of 18 species of duiker, almost all of which are currently at risk. The biggest threat to this species is from illegal hunting, which continues despite international efforts to prevent it.

Duikers are small forest-dwelling antelope with slightly hunched backs. Strikingly patterned animals, this species was named after Mr. F. Jentink, who caught the first recorded specimen during an expedition to West Africa in 1884. The species was officially described and named in 1892, by which time it was recognized as one of the world's rarest antelopes. Indeed, no more were seen for another half century. The lack of sightings was not really surprising, since Jentink's duiker is not only rare, it is also extremely shy and retiring. It only comes out at night and is easily scared.

The name "duiker" comes from the Afrikaans word meaning "diver," and it describes the way in which a nervous antelope darts for cover at the slightest disturbance. Jentink's duiker is highly territorial, with solitary individuals or pairs living well spaced out at low densities. They mark their territories using scent from large glands in the face, and both sexes will defend their patch from other members of the species, using their short horns as weapons.

As the human populations of Liberia, Sierra Leone, and the Ivory Coast extend the boundaries of developed land into previously undisturbed forest habitat, Jentink's duikers have become a more familiar sight. For most endangered animals more sightings could be taken as a promising sign of recovery, but in this case the increased visibility of the Jentink's duiker is more an indication of the growing human pressure on their habitat, forcing them from the forest and out into the open. There are probably fewer duikers alive now than ever before. As forest is cleared by loggers and farmers, the animals are becoming more reliant on low-grade secondary woodland for cover, venturing into bush and fields, and sometimes even raiding crops for food.

Threatened by Hunting

The greatest threat to Jentink's duiker is hunting for bush meat. Being the largest of the duikers, Jentink's is more at risk from hunting than its smaller relatives, although it is officially protected from commercial hunting. Even in areas where the law is understood by local people, it is almost impossible to enforce. The problem is most serious in areas where large numbers

Jentink's duiker hides in forests and thickets by day and emerges to feed at night, when its strikingly patterned coat makes it difficult to see in the moonlight. The female gives birth to one young, which suckles (below) for five months.

See also: Money Problems **1:** 88; Gazelle, Dama **5:** 20; Kudu, Greater **6:** 16

of people come to work in the forests. In Sierra Leone civil war means that soldiers as well as loggers are living off the land, either catching their own meat in the forest or being supplied by local hunters. Until peace returns to the country, there will be little opportunity to promote conservation issues.

At least some of the range of Jentink's duiker is protected; but because the animals live at such low densities, few reserves and national parks are large enough to support a really substantial population. Individuals can apparently live happily in captivity, where they are fed a varied diet of fruit, leaves, and meat. However, since the only two currently held are both males, there is no immediate hope for a captive-breeding program. Improved public education and protection of the animals and their habitats offer the duiker its best chances of survival, but it is difficult to promote such policies in a poor and politically volatile part of the world.

DATA PANEL

Jentink's duiker (squirrel duiker)

Cephalophus jentinki

Family: Bovidae

World population: Fewer than 2,000

Distribution: Sierra Leone, Liberia, Ivory Coast

Habitat: Dense forests and scrub

Size: Length: 4.5 ft (1.4 m); height at shoulder: 30–33 in (75–80 cm). Weight: up to 155 lb (70 kg)

Form: Small, short-horned antelope with short legs and slightly arched back. Coat distinctively patterned: dark head and neck, white collar, grizzled gray back, and pale legs; narrow crest of tufty fur on head

Diet: Mostly plant material, including leaves, shoots, and fruit; some insects, carrion, and birds' eggs

Breeding: Single young born after 7.5-month gestation; weaned at 5 months; female matures at 9–12 months; male at 12–18 months. Life span up to 12 years

Related endangered species: Ader's duiker *(Cephalophus adersi)* EN; Ruwenzori black-fronted duiker *(C. nigrifrons)* EN

Status: IUCN VU; CITES I

Dunnart, Kangaroo Island

Sminthopsis aitkeni

Seen only eight times in a quarter of a century, the Kangaroo Island dunnart is both rare and elusive. Efforts are underway to find out more about the animal so that it can be conserved.

Until the late 1960s there were thought to be no dunnarts of any species living on Kangaroo Island off the coast of South Australia. However, in 1969 a domestic dog captured and killed two specimens of what appeared to be the common dunnart. It was reported that the dog had caught the mouselike animals as they fled from yacca trees that were being felled to make way for farmland. At the time common dunnarts were considered to be relatively abundant and widespread on the mainland of Australia. However, since they had never before been found on Kangaroo Island, the corpses were considered important enough to be sent to the Museum of South Australia in Adelaide.

By the mid-1980s science had progressed sufficiently to allow closely related species to be distinguished by biochemical differences. As a result, many similar-looking animals could now be separated out and given the full species status they deserved. The common dunnart was a worthy candidate for such treatment. When specimens from different parts of Australia were processed in 1984, it became clear that there were, in fact, four species of "common dunnart" that had been grouped together because they looked so similar. Three of them—the common dunnart (from southeastern Australia), the little long-tailed dunnart, and Gilbert's dunnart (both from Western Australia)—appeared to be relatively secure. However, the newly named Kangaroo Island dunnart was an immediate conservation worry because no populations existed anywhere else.

Lack of Information

The Kangaroo Island dunnart appears to live in a variety of natural heathland habitats on the island; but the species is incredibly elusive, and its precise requirements are not known. The lack of sightings can be partly explained by the fact that the animals are

South Australia

New South Wales

AUSTRALIA

Kangaroo Island

Victoria

DATA PANEL

Kangaroo Island dunnart (sooty dunnart)		
Sminthopsis aitkeni	**Size:** Length head/body: 3–4 in (7.6–10 cm); tail: 3.5–4 in (9–10 cm); male about 10% larger than female. Weight: 0.7–0.9 oz (20–25 g)	**Breeding:** Probably similar to common dunnart, with large litters born after short gestation; young weaned at about 2 months
Family: Dasyuridae		**Related endangered species:** Boullanger Island gray-bellied dunnart *(Sminthopsis grisoventer)* CR; Julia Creek dunnart *(S. douglasi)* EN; sandhill dunnart *(S. psammophilla)* EN; Butler's dunnart *(S. butleri)* VU; Queensland common dunnart *(S. murina tatei)* LRnt
World population: Unknown, but tiny	**Form:** Mouselike marsupial with long, tapering snout and long tail; fur grayish tinged with sooty black on back	
Distribution: Kangaroo Island, South Australia		
Habitat: Mallee (scrub) heathland	**Diet:** Probably insectivorous, like the closely related common dunnart	
		Status: IUCN EN; not listed by CITES

See also: Speciation **1:** 26; Research **1:** 84; Mulgara **6:** 94

probably nocturnal. Like some of their mainland relatives, they may also go into a kind of hibernation during food shortages, seeking out secure refuges in which to hide. The absence of more detailed information is not due to a lack of effort. Indeed, there have been several attempts to survey the population using standard live-trapping techniques. So far all that biologists have learned is that the dunnart is rare—and cautious. After numerous trapping attempts only six individuals have been found, bringing the total of recorded specimens to just eight. What is almost certain is that wherever dunnarts live and breed on the island, they are at risk of dying out.

In 1983 laws were passed to protect native Australian vegetation, over 60 percent of which had already been cleared from Kangaroo Island for agriculture. Without knowing more about the dunnart's habitat, it is impossible to judge what effect land clearance might have had on numbers, or to take measures to safeguard its future.

Interim Measures

The manner in which the first Kangaroo Island dunnarts were discovered—they were caught by a domestic dog—showed only too clearly that introduced predators, including pets, are a serious threat to dunnart populations. The fact that such animals did not exist on Kangaroo Island until relatively recently may be the only reason the dunnarts have survived as long as they have. Until more is known about the species, the removal of predators and a complete ban on habitat disruption are the only measures that will have any chance of helping this endangered island mammal.

An extra-long tail *and black-tinted fur are the characteristics that set the Kangaroo Island dunnart apart from its common relative on the mainland. It was only recognized as a distinct species in 1984.*

Eagle, Harpy

Harpia harpyja

The world's most powerful bird of prey, the magnificent harpy eagle—like so many other birds of the New World tropics—suffers badly from hunting and is becoming increasingly disturbed by human encroachment into its rainforest habitat.

The harpy eagle was named after the half-bird, half-woman creatures of ancient Greek mythology, the harpies, who were capable of snatching living things and bearing them out of this world; the name means "one who snatches."

True to its name, the harpy eagle is a swift and powerful hunter. With its incredibly sharp eyesight and hearing, it can locate prey at a considerable distance. The harpy's main targets are sloths: The slow-moving mammals are probably particularly susceptible because they are conspicuous when they climb up into the canopy (rooflike covering of trees) to warm themselves in the morning sun.

The eagle begins its attack by swooping down from its perch high in the trees at impressive speed, weaving neatly between the branches with surprising agility for such a huge bird, thanks to its short, broad, and rounded wings and its long tail. Then, as it closes in on its victim, it suddenly rolls over on its back and, as it hurtles past beneath the sloth, rips the sloth from the branch, unlocking the grip of the mammal's huge claws. Righting itself immediately, the eagle then flies back to the canopy, where it tears up the prey to feed itself or its young. To achieve such a feat, the harpy eagle has the mightiest legs and feet of any bird of prey. Its legs are as thick as a child's wrist and capable of carrying prey almost as heavy as the bird itself. Its sturdy toes are armed with huge, razor-sharp talons.

Human Threats

The main threat facing the harpy eagle is shooting by hunters. Although the birds are generally inconspicuous and spend much of their time high in the trees, their great size and boldness when faced with humans, especially near the nest, makes them highly vulnerable to hunters. It is also likely that the eagles suffer food shortages when hunters kill animals on which they depend for food.

The threat from hunting is particularly acute because harpy eagles are extremely slow breeders. Although the female lays two eggs, one is wasted: As soon as the first chick hatches, she stops incubating the other egg. Also, because each youngster remains dependent on its parents for food and protection for up to a year or more after it has left the nest, a pair of harpy eagles can rear only one offspring at best every third year.

Although harpy eagles are still fairly common in Guyana and the great Amazonian forests, especially in Brazil and Peru, they have been exterminated from large areas of their former range. Some may be able to survive in disturbed areas of forest and even mixed forest and pasture, but harpy eagles are also threatened in the long term by their rainforest habitat continuing to be destroyed or degraded as a result of logging, mining, agriculture, and other developments. The situation is particularly acute in Central America, where the forests are generally smaller and more fragmented. With habitat alteration come roads, which make it so much easier for people, including hunters, to reach previously remote areas where the eagles were once safe.

Conservation

Conservation plans to save the harpy eagle include surveying breeding birds and monitoring nests in parts

See also: Captive Breeding **1:** 87; Eagle, Philippine **4:** 54; Eagle, Spanish Imperial **4:** 56; Kite, Red **6:** 6; Sloth, Maned **9:** 6

The harpy eagle *has rear talons up to 2.8 inches (7 cm) long with which it pierces its prey's vital organs.*

of their range—particularly in Panama and Venezuela—to learn more about their status, distribution, and breeding biology. Satellite transmitters and radios have been attached to young birds so that their movements can be tracked. The data will help show how much territory each bird needs to survive.

A captive-breeding program at the Peregrine Fund's World Center for Birds of Prey in Boise, Idaho, has succeeded in rearing young. The aim is to release birds into areas where, although the species has been lost, suitable habitat remains. Another captive-breeding center is being set up in Panama at the Summit Zoo, not far from Panama City. In the long term, however, it will be essential to control hunting effectively and to reduce the rate of forest destruction by setting up fully protected forest reserves.

DATA PANEL

Harpy eagle

Harpia harpyja

Family: Accipitridae

World population: Estimated at more than 10,000 birds

Distribution: Mexico to northeastern Argentina

Habitat: Mainly large, undisturbed areas of lowland tropical forest

Size: Length: 3–3.5 ft (0.9–1 m); wingspan: up to 6.5 ft (2 m). Weight: male 9–10.5 lb (4–4.8 kg); female 16.8–20 lb (7.6–9 kg)

Form: Large bird of prey with relatively short, broad wings and long tail; head has double crest of stiff feathers; massive, sharply hooked bill; powerful legs and feet. Gray, black, and white plumage. Immatures take 4 years to reach adult plumage; they are duller in coloration with white head

Diet: Mainly tree-dwelling mammals such as sloths; also howler and capuchin monkeys, porcupines, and anteaters. Sometimes such ground-dwelling mammals as agoutis and young brocket deer; birds such as macaws and curassows; reptiles such as snakes and iguanas

Breeding: Builds huge nest up to 5 ft (1.5 m) wide in tall forest trees above the canopy; female lays 2 white eggs, incubated for about 8 weeks; only 1 young survives; fledging takes place at about 5 months

Related endangered species: Philippine eagle (*Pithecophaga jefferyi*)* CR; New Guinea harpy eagle (*Harpyopsis novaeguineae*) VU

Status: LRnt; CITES I and II

Eagle, Philippine

Pithecophaga jefferyi

One of the rarest of the world's birds of prey, the Philippine eagle is in a precarious situation. Its small and rapidly declining population is threatened by forest destruction and fragmentation.

The Philippine eagle is a flagship species for wildlife conservation on four of the Philippine group of islands. Predictions of its imminent extinction have been made since the 1960s, but the species hangs on in the face of immense odds. Conservationists believe that most of the population is equally distributed between the large islands of Luzon and Mindanao (an estimated 105 pairs), while the smaller islands of Samar and Leyte house only an estimated eight pairs between them. However, these figures are based mostly on forest-cover data, and more precise information on numbers is not available.

The Philippine eagle is a huge and powerful predator. It waits on a perch high in the rain forest canopy, looking and listening for the slightest movement or sound that betrays prey beneath. Its relatively short, rounded wings and long tail equip it for weaving deftly among the trees. It often begins a hunt at the top of a hillside and works its way down; it starts the process again when it reaches the bottom.

The Philippine eagle was once known as the monkey-eating eagle. Although it eats various species of monkey, it more often feeds on two cat-sized mammals: the flying lemur and the palm civet. It is likely that the eagle is also an opportunistic hunter, taking different prey according to its availability and abundance. Each pair hunts in a large territory of about 23 to 38 square miles (60 to 100 sq. km). As in other eagle species, the pairs mate for life.

Lost Forest

As with so many other species, the main threat facing the Philippine eagle is the relentless destruction of its habitat. Every year some of the remaining primary forest on the islands is felled for timber: The great

DATA PANEL

Philippine eagle (monkey-eating eagle)

Pithecophaga jefferyi

Family: Accipitridae

World population: 350–650 birds; possibly only 226 mature adults

Distribution: Philippine islands of Luzon, Leyte, Mindanao, and Samar

Habitat: Primary dipterocarp (hardwood) rain forest on steep slopes; sometimes lives among secondary growth and gallery forest along riverbanks and floodplains. Occurs from the lowlands to 5,900 ft (1,800 m)

Size: Length: 34–40 in (86–102 cm); wingspan: about 6.5 ft (2 m). Weight: 10.3–17.6 lb (4.7–8 kg)

Form: Huge eagle with large, arched, powerfully hooked blue bill. Dark area around eyes (which have pale blue-gray irises) contrasts with buff crown and nape; long, spiky, black-streaked feathers form scruffy crest; cheeks, throat, underparts, and underwings white; upperparts and upperwings dark brown; legs and feet yellow

Diet: Tree-dwelling mammals such as flying lemurs, palm civets, monkeys, and flying squirrels; also tree-dwelling birds, including hornbills, owls, and hawks; bats, monitor lizards, and snakes

Breeding: Female lays 1 white egg in huge stick nest high in canopy of tall tree, usually on an epiphytic fern (one that grows on another plant). Both sexes incubate for about 9 weeks; eaglet fledges after about 5 months; remains dependent on parents for another year or more

Related endangered species: New Guinea harpy eagle (*Harpyopsis novaeguineae*) VU; harpy eagle (*Harpia harpyja*)* LRnt

Status: IUCN CR; CITES I

See also: Habitat Loss 1: 38; Eagle, Harpy 4: 52; Eagle, Spanish Imperial 4: 56; Lemur, Philippine Flying 6: 24

dipterocarp (tall hardwood) trees growing there are a major source of tropical timber for the rest of the world. When the loggers leave, settlers who practice "slash-and-burn" cultivation frequently move in. Slash-and-burn agriculture produces poor-quality, weed-infested grassland with bamboo or other scrub in place of a rich forest and is of little value to the eagles.

With the increasing numbers of people moving into the forests, it is probable that only 3,560 square miles (9,220 sq. km) of forest remain. Even national parks are severely affected; in Mount Apo National Park, for instance, over 50 percent of the original forest has disappeared.

Other threats facing the Philippine eagle include hunting by local people for food or trophies and, until recently, the capture of young for sale to zoos and the cage-bird trade. Plans for mining operations have also caused concern. There is evidence that the eagles accumulate pesticides from their prey in their body, a factor that is likely to affect their breeding success—a serious problem in a species that produces only one young every two years, at most.

Last Hope

Over the past 30 to 40 years various conservation initiatives have been launched to assure the future of the Philippine eagle. Plans include protective legislation, surveys, captive breeding, public awareness programs, and a sustainable agriculture project designed to improve conditions for both eagles and local people. However, relatively little is still known of the bird's ecology, and the work has been hampered at intervals by natural disasters and serious political unrest, as well as by the difficult nature of the remote habitats the eagle favors.

The Philippine eagle *perches high up in the rain forest canopy, watching for prey. Plans for its conservation include a campaign to foster national pride in the bird. If that is successful, the eagle may yet avoid extinction in the wild.*

Eagle, Spanish Imperial

Aquila adalberti

One of the world's rarest birds of prey, the Spanish imperial eagle was thought to be in recovery in the early 1980s, but recently numbers have declined again. Like many other birds of prey, it has come into increasing conflict with the demands of people and is now seriously threatened.

At the beginning of the 20th century the Spanish imperial eagle was still relatively common and widespread. It could be found over most of Spain in areas of dry, uncultivated habitat. It also bred in Portugal and Morocco.

Today the species has disappeared from much of its range as a result of the loss and fragmentation of its forest habitat. By the 1960s the Spanish imperial eagle was almost extinct, with only 30 pairs recorded. Conservationists tried a new rescue technique. First, they located nests with three or four eaglets. The last chicks to hatch often die as a result of the so-called Cain and Abel conflict. The "conflict" describes the tendency of the stronger nestlings to kill their younger siblings—as Cain killed his brother Abel in the biblical story. Sometimes the weaker siblings starve, since they are not strong enough to compete for the food brought by their parents.

Rescued eaglets were then put into nests with only a single chick. The number of surviving fledglings increased by up to 43 percent. From the early 1980s the species started to recover, and an average of five new breeding pairs appeared each year until 1994. Unfortunately, the population has since declined from 148 pairs in 1994 to 131 pairs in 1998. More significantly, even in major strongholds breeding success has plummeted.

Threats to Survival

Spanish imperial eagles need large areas of open forest with scattered trees or clumps of woodland for nesting and rough grassland or open ground for hunting. The birds avoid areas that have been irrigated for crops and site their nests well away from settlements, roads, and other developments. Wild places are increasingly difficult to find as more people move into undeveloped areas. The eagles are sensitive to disturbance, which can affect their breeding success.

Another major factor affecting the eagle's success is the availability

---

DATA PANEL

Spanish imperial eagle (Adalbert's eagle)

Aquila adalberti

Family: Accipitridae

World population: About 260 birds

Distribution: Breeds in central and southwestern Spain, in the Sierras of Guadarrama and Gredos, the plains of the Tajo and Tiétar Rivers, the central hills of Extremadura, Montes de Toledo, the Alcudia Valley, Sierra Morena, and the Guadalquivir marshes; also Salamanca and Málaga

Habitat: Open, wooded areas away from irrigated and cultivated farmland; high mountain slopes; hills and plains; sand dunes and alluvial plains

Size: Length: 29.5–33 in (75–84 cm); wingspan: 6–8 ft (1.8–2.4 m). Weight: 5.5–7.7 lb (2.5–3.5 kg)

Form: Huge bird of prey with dark plumage. Brown-black coloration with white "shoulders," pale-golden nape,

and pale-gray base to upper tail. Juveniles have rust-colored plumage that fades to pale buff; dark flight feathers; white fringes to wing coverts (feathers covering the flight feathers)

Diet: Mainly mammals, especially rabbits; also pigeons, waterbirds, gamebirds, and members of the crow family; occasionally snakes and lizards. Also dead cows and other grazing mammals

Breeding: Large stick nest built in tree; female usually lays 2–4 brown-blotched whitish eggs that are incubated for about 6 weeks; young fledge in about 10 weeks

Related endangered species: Imperial eagle (*Aquila heliaca*) VU; greater spotted eagle (*A. clanga*) VU

Status: IUCN VU; CITES I and II

See also: Disease **1:** 55; A Tale of Two Eagles **1:** 94; Eagle, Philippine **4:** 54; Kestrel, Lesser **5:** 94; Kite, Red **6:** 6

of rabbits. Rabbits usually form more than half of the eagle's total prey—in some places as much as 70 percent. However, the viral disease myxomatosis, deliberately introduced to control rabbit populations in 1957, was very effective. In a few areas eagles switched to hunting alternative prey. It is likely that many pairs were forced to stop breeding due to the shortage of rabbits. Another viral disease—hemorrhagic pneumonia—has added to the drop in rabbit numbers: in some areas by 80 percent.

Deliberate and accidental poisoning of the eagles is another cause of the bird's decline, especially in hunting preserves where game animals are commercially exploited. Carcasses baited with powerful poisons are now a significant cause of death. Such traps kill other species, too, including domestic dogs. Between 1989 and 1999 at least 57 Spanish imperial eagles died from poisoning—probably more than by any other means.

The eagles are also vulnerable to electrocution by power cables. Inexperienced juveniles are most at risk, especially when their plumage is wet. There are more deaths when power lines are sited away from roads and in areas where there are large numbers of rabbits.

Conservation Plans

Although 60 percent of the breeding population lives in 20 protected areas, the species still needs urgent help. A coordinated conservation plan is being implemented. Priorities include annual censuses of the breeding population, protecting nesting areas, increasing the rabbit population, working toward the elimination of poisoning, and surveying and modifying power lines to prevent electrocution.

The Spanish imperial eagle *is a huge bird of prey with a wingspan of between 6 and 8 feet (1.8 and 2.4 m).*

Earthworm, Giant Gippsland

Megascolides australis

One of the largest earthworms in the world, the giant gippsland earthworm was discovered in 1878. Its large size and secretive habits have made it vulnerable to changes in land use resulting from the development of agricultural land from natural forest.

The giant Gippsland earthworm belongs to the Phylum Annelida, the segmented worms, which includes earthworms, ragworms, and leeches. Named after the area of Australia that is its home, it is found only in Gippsland, a fertile region of southeastern Victoria that extends along the coast from Melbourne to the New South Wales border.

The giant Gippsland earthworm lives in permanent and elaborate burrows, spending all its life underground. There it feeds on the roots of plants and on other organic matter in the soil. Most earthworm species deposit their waste material as obvious casts on the surface, but this species leaves its cast material below ground.

As a result of its exclusively underground life the giant Gippsland earthworm is difficult to study. Consequently, many aspects of its biology are unknown. We do know that its body is divided up into between 300 to 500 visible segments. The head and front third of the body are a dark purple color, while the remainder, behind the "saddle," is a pinkish-gray.

Giant Gippsland earthworms are not easily kept in captivity, and because of their large size and fragility they are easily damaged or killed by scientists and farmers alike.

Patchy Distribution

The distribution of the giant Gippsland earthworm was previously much wider than it is today. When European settlers arrived in the 18th century, they transformed large areas of native forest into pasture for the dairy industry. The disturbances associated with this proved very damaging to the worms.

Today giant Gippsland earthworms tend to be restricted to steep hillsides and valleys where the soils cannot be plowed. Any activities that affect the moisture content and drainage of the soil can also be bad news for the worms. Building roads and dams,

New South Wales
AUSTRALIA
Victoria
Tasmania

DATA PANEL

Giant Gippsland earthworm

Megascolides australis

Family: Megascolecidae

World population: Unknown

Distribution: Restricted to about 40 square miles (100 sq. km) of land in Gippsland, Victoria, Australia

Habitat: Burrows in organically rich soils

Size: Length: 31 in (80 cm); diameter 0.8 in (2 cm)

Form: Typical segmented worm; a definite head and 300–500 segments each with chaetae (bristles); well-developed respiratory and vascular system

Diet: Plant tissue and organic matter in soil

Breeding: Worms are hermaphrodite, but 2 individuals are required for fertilization to occur. Mating takes place in spring and early summer. Individuals lay a single amber-colored egg capsule containing 1 embryo, which takes

about 12 months to hatch. The earthworms are presumed to reach adulthood about 4.5 years after hatching. Adults may be long-lived

Related endangered species: Washington giant earthworm (*Driloleirus americanus*) VU; Oregon giant earthworm (*D. macelfreshi*) VU

Status: IUCN VU; not listed by CITES

See also: Pasture 1: 38; Saving the Habitats 1: 88; Leech, Medicinal 6: 20

The giant Gippsland earthworm, *like other earthworms, is beneficial to the fertility of soil. However, more needs to be known about this elusive and fragile creature so that it can be protected.*

trenching, and laying cables are all damaging activities. Natural seasonal fluctuations of moisture content govern the normal movement of the worms within the soil.

Recent surveys of southern and western Gippsland have shown that the giant earthworm is restricted to about 40 square miles (100 sq. km) of land in an area bounded approximately by Loch, Korumburra, and Warragul. Much of this land is unsuitable, and the giant earthworm's distribution is very patchy. The population density of the adult worms within the acceptable areas is usually low, about two individuals per 35 cubic feet (two per cubic meter). The worms are mostly found in blue-gray clay soils on flats by the banks of streams or along ditches and watercourses where the slopes face a southwesterly direction.

Like all earthworms, the giant Gippsland worms have beneficial effects on the quality of the soil in which they live, contributing to an increase in its organic content and assisting aeration and increasing fertility. The giant Gippsland earthworm has become part of the folklore of southern Gippsland, and many landowners speak with pride about its presence on their properties.

Conservation

Conserving the giant Gippsland earthworm is difficult. Retaining natural vegetation alongside streams as well as on steep slopes and in valleys and keeping out livestock by fencing the remaining earthworm habitats are both thought to be helpful measures. However, such strategies rely heavily on the cooperation of private landowners and farmers who may need help in identifying the parts of their properties that accommodate the giant earthworms. One issue that has recently made this more difficult is the splitting up of larger properties into smaller ones used for small-scale farming.

Echidna, Long-Beaked

Zaglossus bruijni

The long-beaked echidna is a reclusive animal that feeds mainly on the worms and small grubs it finds in the wet forest leaf litter. A slow breeder, it is hunted for food and suffers from habitat loss.

The long-beaked echidna is an egg-laying mammal that inhabits the thick, humid forests of New Guinea, an island north of Australia. It lives alone, sheltering in a burrow or other hideout during the day. Since it seems to be active largely at night and is rare, even in undisturbed habitats, it is difficult to study, and little is known of its habits. A 1998 report suggests that there may be three species of long-beaked echidna, but one is known from only a single specimen and may already be extinct.

Unlike its cousin the short-beaked echidna, which feeds extensively on ants and termites, the long-beaked echidna seems to specialize in eating worms. It seeks them out by poking its long, curved snout into rotting wood or under moss and leaves. The jaws do not open far, and they are weak and have no teeth, so the food must be swallowed without being chewed. Worms, beetle larvae, and grubs of all sorts are abundant in wet forest leaf litter, so there is normally sufficient food even for such a large creature.

Rare Animals

When the forests are cut down, the ground dries out, and the staple foods of the echidna's diet become less abundant. Felling trees also removes the availability of rotten wood, a vital source of invertebrate food. Large areas of forest have been cleared in New Guinea to make way for new villages, roads, mines, and farms. Still more has been felled for timber. The echidnas can now only survive in the remote areas where they are not troubled by such developments. They appear to have become extinct in the central highlands within the last 50 years, and they are no longer found in most of the northern areas of New Guinea.

Echidnas have been hunted by specially trained dogs and their meat is highly prized by native people as a rare delicacy to be eaten at traditional feasts. Echidnas cannot climb, run fast, or attack predators, so they are easily captured. It is said that echidnas live at an average density of 4 per square mile (1 or 2 per sq. km).

DATA PANEL

Long-beaked echidna

Zaglossus bruijni

Family: Tachyglossidae

World population: Unknown, probably low thousands

Distribution: New Guinea (Papua New Guinea and West Irian, a province of Indonesia)

Habitat: Various habitats from lowland tropical jungles to mountain forests and grasslands at more than 13,000 ft (4,000 m) above sea level

Size: Length: 18–30 in (45–77 cm); height at shoulder: about 10 in (25 cm). Weight: 11–22 lb (5–10 kg)

Form: A small animal covered in short, thick spines and dense, black hair. Long, tubular, downcurved snout. Feet have large claws; hind ones point sideways; walks slowly with rolling gait

Diet: Invertebrates, mainly earthworms

Breeding: Details unknown, but probably lays 1 egg per year in July; egg is incubated in temporary pouch on the mother's belly. Young fed on milk for several months before becoming independent. A long-beaked echidna has lived more than 30 years in captivity; life span in the wild unknown

Related endangered species: Short-beaked echidna *(Tachyglossus aculeatus multiaculeatus)* LRnt

Status: IUCN EN; CITES II

New Guinea
INDONESIA
PAPUA NEW GUINEA
AUSTRALIA

See also: Habitat Loss **1:** 38; Platypus **7:** 82; Tree-Kangaroo, Goodfellow's **10:** 4

Multiplying this by the area of suitable habitat suggests that there may be over 300,000 animals in total, but such a figure is unlikely. In a sample of skulls from the remains of several thousand native animals killed for consumption in traditional feasts there was only one long-beaked echidna.

The long-beaked echidna breeds very slowly, producing only a single baby each year. The young are extremely vulnerable and almost defenseless for many months (apart from their spines). As a result of its slow breeding rate, the species is unable to sustain heavy losses. Echidnas are not at risk from large natural predators since there are none living on New Guinea. Consequently, their spines have evolved to offer the animal only limited protection. However, introduced dogs and increasing numbers of people present

The long-beaked echidna *is one of the few egg-laying mammals. In this young echidna (above) the black fur is not yet fully developed. The spines show up clearly in the photograph, taken at night with flash illumination.*

dangers that the animal cannot withstand. Long-beaked echidnas have full legal protection, but the law is not always enforced in remote areas.

Little is known about the breeding biology of echidnas; outside New Guinea specimens are kept in only one zoo in Sydney, Australia. Even the short-beaked echidna has rarely bred in captivity, so there seems to be little prospect of developing a "safety net" of captive-bred echidnas as an insurance against extinction. Maximum protection in the Lorenz National Park and other nature reserves in New Guinea is vital.

Eel, Lesser Spiny

Macrognathus aral

The lesser spiny eel is relatively abundant in India, but populations have severely declined in Sri Lanka, where it is now only found in four locations. The reasons for the population decline are not known, and neither is the potential threat to other spiny eel populations elsewhere.

The only thing that spiny eels have in common with the "true" eels is their cylindrical and elongated body shape. Otherwise, they are quite different. True eels (family Anguillidae of the order Anguilliformes) are long, slender fish known for the long-distance migrations undertaken by at least two species—the North American eel and the European eel—to and from their spawning grounds. Although they are freshwater eels, they spawn in the Sargasso Sea, a calm area in the North Atlantic between the West Indies and the Azores. True eels produce leptocephali—slender, transparent larvae that do not resemble adults. They gradually undergo metamorphosis to juveniles on their journey back to freshwater rivers. On reaching maturity years later, they return to the Sargasso Sea to spawn.

Unlike true eels, spiny eels are freshwater fish that live, breed, and die in rivers. Their larvae do not go through the leptocephalus stage; young spiny eels are tiny replicas of their parents.

There are two groups of fish known as spiny eels: the freshwater fish of the family Mastacembelidae and the deep-sea fish of the family Notacanthidae—a little-known group. In the Mastacembelidae, which includes the lesser spiny eel, there are about 70 species in four genera. Two genera—namely *Aethiomastacembelus* and *Caecomastacembelus* (sometimes called *Afromastacembelus*)—are found in Africa, and the other two—*Mastacembelus* and *Macrognathus*—are found in Asia.

The common name of spiny eels reflects the series of small spines that extend for varying distances along

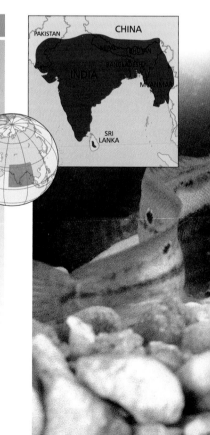

DATA PANEL

Lesser spiny eel

Macrognathus aral

Family: Mastacembelidae

World population: Relatively abundant in parts of its range, but close to extinction (or extinct) in Sri Lanka

Distribution: Indian subcontinent, Myanmar (Burma), and Sri Lanka

Habitat: Mainly still or slow-flowing waters with marginal vegetation and muddy or silty bottoms

Size: Length: up to 12 in (30 cm) reported

Form: Elongated, slender body with series of small, isolated spines running down the back up to the front edge of the soft part of the dorsal (back) fin. Snout tapered, ending in 3 fleshy lobes. Dorsal

(back), caudal (tail), and anal (belly) fins are separate (they are fused in some other spiny eels); there are no pelvic (hip) fins. Two brown stripes separated by yellowy stripes run the length of the body; dorsal fin has 2 or more ocelli (eyelike markings): black spots edged in yellow

Diet: Aquatic insects and other invertebrates

Breeding: Little is known about courtship and breeding behavior. Eggs are laid on vegetation and apparently abandoned. Hatching takes place in 1 or 2 days

Related endangered species: None

Status: IUCN DD; not listed by CITES

See also: Populations **1:** 20; Research **1:** 84; Rasbora, Vateria Flower **8:** 22

the back and up to the front edge of the soft part of the dorsal (back) fin. These are used in defense when a fish feels threatened. Some species, for instance, will wriggle backward when picked up, giving the handler a nasty and painful surprise with the spines. The backward movement is probably an instinctive reaction that in the wild would allow the fish to bury itself rapidly in the soft mud or silt on the riverbed and so escape from danger.

Abundant or Endangered?

General information about the family of spiny eels is readily available, but detailed data on many species, including the lesser spiny eel, is more difficult to find. It is known that the species is relatively abundant on the Indian subcontinent and in Myanmar (Burma). Indeed, Indian specimens are regularly exported for home aquaria and are reported to be "ideal aquarium inhabitants." Along with other members of the family, the lesser spiny eel is considered a delicious food in India, and at one time it was also thought to be a delicacy in Sri Lanka.

The collapse of Sri Lanka's lesser spiny eel population has led to a growing belief that it could be extinct in this part of its range. However, occasional reports in recent years have located isolated specimens at a few sites, which suggests that the "extinct" label may be a little premature. In 1991 researchers reported that they had found the species in four locations. Since sightings do occur, the species is regarded as rare rather than extinct. Nevertheless, the lesser spiny eel was once abundant enough for it to be collected from rice paddies or even on baited hook and line.

Equally worrying is the fact that the cause, or causes, of the decline in the populations is unknown. There are no indications that overcollection for consumption or home aquaria is a contributory factor. On the other hand, the use of pesticides in farming and changes brought about through agriculture are thought to have been detrimental to the eel's habitat. However, no detailed studies have been carried out.

It is clear that the lesser spiny eel is in a precarious state. While the species as a whole is not under threat, the Sri Lankan population undoubtedly is. Since the decline has been so dramatic and is so little understood, it raises questions about the long-term stability of the other lesser spiny eel populations.

The lesser spiny eel *resembles the true eel, but is not related to it. It is an elongated fish that is nocturnal and burrows in the riverbed during most of the day.*

Elephant, African

Loxodonta africana

The African elephant is the largest land mammal on earth. It is a remarkable creature, not only because of its size and bulk, but also because of its intelligence, memory, and behavior.

The statistics surrounding the African elephant are as impressive as the animal itself: It is the world's largest land mammal and has the longest gestation of any animal (660 days—nearly two years). An adult elephant can drink between 15 and 20 gallons (70 and 90 l) of water a day and eat about 330 pounds (150 kg) of food. Despite its size and weight, however, an African elephant can reach speeds of 25 miles per hour (40 km/h) when charging or fleeing.

The elephant's distinctive trunk has many functions. It is used for feeding, carrying, spraying water or dust to cool itself, making sounds, greeting other elephants, threatening, stroking, and even as a pacifier for baby elephants to suck on. Elephants have long tusks made of ivory that they use for fighting and digging; they flap their large ears to keep cool in the African heat.

The Romans wrote about elephants living on the Mediterranean coast of North Africa, but today African elephants can only be found on the savanna grasslands and forests south of the Sahara Desert. There they feed on the grasses and foliage, sometimes ripping trees out with their trunks and stripping them of bark and leaves. The female elephants (cows) live in herds with their calves and close female relatives. The herd is led by the oldest female elephant, called the matriarch. Male elephants (bulls) leave the herd when they reach puberty. They live alone or in small bachelor groups, only joining a herd again to mate.

Elephants live for about 70 years. They are social animals and have been known to work together—particularly in times of danger—to help sick or injured family members. They are also thought to grieve for their dead relatives.

African elephants *flap their large ears to keep themselves cool. This elephant is red from dust bathing—another way of cooling off.*

DATA PANEL

African elephant

Loxodonta africana

Family: Elephantidae

World population: Up to 543,000

Distribution: Sub-Saharan Africa

Habitat: Savanna grasslands; forests

Size: Length: up to 16.4 ft (5 m); height at shoulder: up to 10.8 ft (3.3 m); males 10% bigger than females. Weight: male up to 6.7 tons (6 tonnes); female up to 3.3 tons (2.9 tonnes)

Form: Huge gray-black body with columnlike legs, large head, large ears, long tusks, and a flexible trunk; little hair on skin

Diet: Grasses, tree leaves, and bark

Breeding: Breeds at 13 or 14 years old; gestation of nearly 2 years. Calves every 3–4 years in wet season. May live up to 70 years

Related endangered species: Asian elephant (*Elephas maximus*)* EN

Status: IUCN EN; CITES I, II, and III, according to country location

See also: Hunting 1: 42; Elephant, Asian 4: 66

African elephant populations have fallen quite dramatically. At the beginning of the 20th century there were many millions of elephants; in 1970 there were 2 million, and today there are probably fewer than half a million. They have few natural predators; their most dangerous enemies are humans.

Trade and Land

Ivory from elephant tusks is a prized material traditionally used to make carvings and jewelry. The trade in ivory began seriously in the 17th century, when Arab traders hunted elephants in West Africa. The invention of guns, and in particular the rifle, meant that hunters could kill animals more efficiently. African elephants are now protected in many countries, and there is an official ban on trade in ivory.

However, there is still a strong demand for the tusks, and illegal poaching is widespread.

Elephants are also threatened by loss of habitat. As the growing human population of Africa demands more land for expanding cities and for farmland, the elephants' habitat has shrunk, limiting their access to food. This can bring them into conflict with humans, since elephants may be driven by hunger to raid crops.

After pressure by conservation organizations the African elephant was put on Appendix I of CITES in 1989, banning international trade in the species and its products. However, several African countries want to continue trading to earn money for conservation.

Conservation groups run projects in Africa strengthening elephant conservation through anti-poaching patrols, education, and trade controls. They also work with local people to reduce conflict between elephants and humans and to promote the benefits of elephants to the local tourist industry.

Elephant, Asian

Elephas maximus

Asian elephants are valued as working animals so they will probably never become extinct. However, wild populations face serious threats.

The Asian elephant is smaller than the African elephant. Found across Southeast Asia, the Asian elephant has already died out in the eastern and western ends of its former range. There are a few hundred Asian elephants in the world's zoos, but few are bred in captivity.

Unlike their African cousins, Asian elephants have for centuries been trained and used as draft (working) animals. Today there are over 10,000 Asian elephants trained for heavy tasks. Ironically, they are used to help drag out felled trees from the forest, the environment on which wild Asian elephants depend.

Huge areas of forest have already been cut down, and losses continue all the time. With the destruction of the forests remnant elephant populations get split into smaller groups that become isolated from each other. In order to meet and breed, it is often necessary to cross developed land, with all the dangers that entails. In a project in Indonesia some elephants that became isolated in this way were actively driven out to join with others in a larger area of habitat.

Elephants need a lot of space: An individual's home range is often up to 15 square miles (40 sq. km) and sometimes over 116 square miles (300 sq. km) in southern India.

The animals need to drink over 11 gallons (50 liters) of water a day, so it is essential that they live near rivers or lakes—exactly the type of land that is considered ideal for agricultural use. Replacing the forests with farmland gives the elephants little choice but to raid the new crops such as bananas and sugarcane. As a result, farmers are inclined to shoot and snare the elephants.

Asian elephants *live in small family groups of females (cows) and their young; most bulls live in bachelor herds. There are about 27,000 elephants in India, but of them only about 1,500 are adult "tuskers." This means that ivory poaching even on a small scale could unbalance populations.*

Elephants need to eat at least 300 lb (150 kg) of plants every day. Such quantities are only available naturally in the lush tropical forests. Even in the fastest-growing forests the elephants need to move around in order to find sufficient food. The animals migrate seasonally between different feeding areas to overcome food shortages during the dry season. However, such movements are now prevented by

See also: War **1:** 47; Why Are Mammals at Risk? **1:** 61; Elephant, African **4:** 64

roads and farmland. Even national parks may not be large enough to accommodate populations of elephants all year round, so special dispersal "corridors" have been created to link areas of forest and enable elephants to migrate seasonally between them. (The Kallar Jaccanari corridor, for example, links the 4,000 elephants of the northern and southern Nilghiri Biosphere Reserve in southern India.) The corridors have to be about 8 miles (13 km) wide.

Wasteful Killing

Shooting and snaring for ivory have been a threat to the Asian elephant for centuries, although the females do not have tusks, and the males sometimes lack

them. (The African elephant has always been under greater threat from hunting for tusks.) Trading in ivory is now forbidden under the CITES agreement.

A new threat to the Asian elephant is the millions of land mines left in the jungles of Cambodia, Vietnam, and other Southeast Asian countries during wars in the 20th century. In Sri Lanka it is estimated that each year about 20 elephants die after stepping on land mines.

Elephant-Shrew, Golden-Rumped

Rhynchocyon chrysopygus

The golden-rumped elephant-shrew and the insects on which it feeds are threatened by habitat loss and disturbance. There is also a threat from increasing numbers of domestic dogs.

The golden-rumped elephant-shrew is a strange-looking creature with long legs, a bright-yellow rump, and a long, flexible nose. It is an unusual insectivore in that it is active almost entirely during the day, rather than at night. The animal bounds about under the cover of dense scrub, using its paws and long probing snout to unearth beetles from under stones and logs. It sometimes seizes grasshoppers and locusts or giant millipedes, and ants, termites, and earthworms are also included in its diet. The elephant-shrew depends on the moist conditions found in dense, shady scrub, where the bushes and trees keep their leaves all year round and shield the soil and its invertebrates from the intense heat of the sun.

The golden-rumped elephant-shrew creates additional shelter by making a shallow depression in the ground and covering it with a large pile of leaves about 3 feet (1 m) wide. A single shrew builds and maintains at least 10 such shelters within its territory; it builds in the morning, when the leaves are damp and easy to pack into tight, dense heaps that it thumps into place with its feet. The mound serves as a shelter for sleeping in and a nest in which to give birth and raise the single baby; female elephant-shrews give birth every two to three months. The mound also offers safety from birds of prey and other predators.

The right conditions for building the shelters are probably the most important requirements in the elephant shrew's habitat. If disturbed in its shelter, perhaps by a snake, an elephant-shrew will leap into action, rushing off at speed down a system of well-used trails. Elephant-shrews are highly territorial; territories average about 4 acres (1.7 ha) in area and are carefully patrolled every day. The shrews chase off intruders and often fight with each other, inflicting severe bites on their opponent's rump. However, the skin on the rump is specially thickened, so the wounds are rarely serious.

A Limited Habitat

The golden-rumped elephant-shrew is found in only two small areas of dense evergreen bush in Kenya, East Africa. Bush clearance for house construction and agricultural development is a threat to the habitat, which is naturally restricted to a narrow strip of coastal land. Other problems include domestic animals, such as goats and dogs. Goats browse the dense undergrowth and

DATA PANEL

Golden-rumped elephant-shrew

Rhynchocyon chrysopygus

Family: Macroscelididae

World population: Unknown, perhaps only hundreds

Distribution: Eastern Kenya

Habitat: Dry, evergreen thickets

Size: Length head/body: 9.3–12.5 in (23.5–31.5 cm); tail: 7.5–10.5 in (19–26.3 cm). Weight: 14.2–15.5 oz (408–440g)

Form: Long-legged, dark-brown animal about the size of a rabbit; bright yellow rump; long, flexible nose

Diet: Large insects, spiders, millipedes, and occasionally worms

Breeding: Single young born at any time of year; 4 or 5 births per year. Life span 4–5 years

Related endangered species: Black and rufous, or zanj, elephant shrew (*Rhynchocyon petersi*) EN; Somali elephant shrew (*Elephantulus revoili*) EN; 4 other species of elephant shrew listed as Vulnerable

Status: IUCN EN; not listed by CITES

See also: Habitat Loss **1:** 38; Natural Disasters **1:** 57; Mole-Rat, Giant **6:** 84

open it up, removing the shelter needed by the elephant-shrews and their prey. At the same time, dogs roam around elephant-shrew habitat, chasing small animals and digging up and destroying the elephant-shrew's leaf-mound shelters.

In the dry season fires are an additional hazard, destroying the vegetation and killing many of the large insects and other prey on which the elephant-shrews feed. Giant millipedes are particularly vulnerable to bush fires and—as with the insects caught in the fire—it can be many months before their numbers recover.

One population of golden-rumped elephant-shrews is based around the Gedi Ruins National Park, a popular tourist attraction near Mombassa. Even here

The golden-rumped elephant-shrew *is a distinctive creature that is typical of a coastal bush habitat. It is rabbit-sized and highly active during the daytime.*

in the relative security of a protected area the shrews are seriously threatened by dogs from the local villages. Fortunately, the region has extensive areas of ancient limestone over which thick scrub grows. Crops will not flourish where the limestone comes close to the surface, so the area is unlikely to be cleared for agriculture. The limestone also has lots of natural holes in it where the elephant-shrews can hide from danger. Nevertheless, the total area of remaining habitat is small, as is the population of golden-rumped elephant-shrews.

Emerald, Orange-Spotted

Oxygastra curtisii

The orange-spotted emerald is extinct in Britain as a result of sewage pollution of its last surviving breeding areas. Although it is still found in low densities in some parts of Europe, its populations are vulnerable to the effects of agriculture and other human activities on its aquatic habitat.

The orange-spotted emerald is a dragonfly species that is now extinct in Britain. It was finally extinguished from the British fauna when a sewage leak polluted its last known habitat in southwestern England. However, it remains in low numbers in western and southern Europe and North Africa. In common with its close relative the damselfly, the dragonfly also depends on fresh water for the completion of its life cycle.

Both dragonflies and damselflies have large, paired eyes that are the most conspicuous structures on their heads, and in the dragonflies the eyes are so large that they virtually meet in the midline. Damselfly eyes are not quite as large, but eyesight is important to both groups. Flying dragonflies can apparently detect moving objects at distances of 39 feet (12 m). When hunting, most individuals patrol fixed beats or hunting grounds, pausing to rest with their wings outstretched on favored resting points that are frequently revisited. Damselflies, on the other hand, rest with their wings partly folded. The shape of the wings also helps distinguish between the two types. Dragonflies have hind wings that are broader than the forewings, and both pairs taper only slightly where they meet the body. The fore and hind wings of damselflies are the same size and show a conspicuous taper just before they join the body.

Territorial

Adult dragonflies spend some of their time near water, but may travel for long distances while they are hunting for prey. Their prey takes the form of small insects, especially other flies and mosquitoes that are caught on the wing. Any male that detects another male of the same species trespassing on his beat will engage him in a fight, and broken legs and torn wings are sometimes sustained in such encounters.

Occasionally, dragonflies engage in migrations or travel for long distances. Two species from continental Europe have been recorded venturing over the sea into southern Britain. However, salt water is not liked by dragonflies for breeding purposes, and only a few species can tolerate brackish (slightly salty) water. Males usually mate with females of the same species that enter their territory, and the mating and egg-laying process is similar to that shown

DATA PANEL

Orange-spotted emerald

Oxygastra curtisii

Family: Corduliidae

World population: Unknown

Distribution: Northwestern and central Europe

Habitat: Rivers, streams, and ponds

Size: Length: about 1.7 in (4.5 cm); wingspan: 2.6 in (6.5 cm)

Form: Adult: typical dragonfly head with conspicuous eyes; long body with 2 pairs of wings, hind wings broader than forewings. Larva: wingless aquatic insect; head with retractile jaws; tail lacks external gill filaments

Diet: Adults feed on small insects, including mosquitoes. Nymphs (larvae) feed on small aquatic animals such as other insect larvae

Breeding: Male looks for females in spring. After courtship and copulation eggs are laid underwater in water plants. Free-living larvae hatch and may feed for many weeks before emerging to molt as adult dragonflies

Related endangered species: Ohio emerald dragonfly (*Somatochlora hineana*) EN; banded bog-skimmer dragonfly (*Williamsonia lintneri*) VU; Calvert's emerald (*S. calverti*) LRnt

Status: IUCN VU; not listed by CITES

by damselflies. After mating the female lays her eggs in the tissues of aquatic plants, where they hatch into predatory aquatic larvae. Again there are similarities between the habits and lifestyles of dragonfly larvae and damselfly larvae. However, dragonfly larvae are generally plumper than damselfly larvae and lack the three external terminal gills of damselfly larvae. The gills of the dragonfly larvae are internal.

Adult orange-spotted emeralds *hunt in woodlands, around lakes, and along riverbanks. They take their insect prey—including mosquitoes and other flies—on the wing.*

Halting the Decline

It is ironic that despite increasing environmental awareness, current pressures from agriculture, building, and infrastructure development continue to exclude established species from their typical habitats: It is the dragonflies' need for specific conditions for reproduction that makes them vulnerable to any kind of disturbance to their aquatic habitat. However, while humans are largely responsible for the decline in orange-spotted dragonfly numbers, there is also much that can be done to help protect the species. For example, restoring water bodies, digging ponds, and preventing plant overgrowth are some of the steps that can be taken to preserve the quality of aquatic habitats. It is also vital that the consequences of

sewage and industrial pollution are clearly understood and that recreational sources of pollution, from boats and vacation homes, for example, are prevented.

One of the difficulties facing conservationists is that different dragonfly species have different freshwater requirements. Some like running water, while others prefer still water or wetlands, including bogs. The effects of development and its associated drainage of such habitats are different in every case.

Dragonflies have been frequenting water bodies since the Carboniferous period 300 million years ago. In the Jurassic period (about 210 million years ago) there were dragonflies similar to those of today. It is unthinkable that future generations should not see dragonflies like the orange-spotted emerald.

Ferret, Black-Footed

Mustela nigripes

Not long ago black-footed ferrets did not exist in the wild. The wiping out of prairie dog burrows in which the animals lodged started their decline. Today captive-bred stock are being reintroduced into the wild, but the population will probably never reach its original size.

The black-footed ferret was probably never abundant. Nonetheless, it used to be found across a broad swathe of the American short grass prairies, from Texas to beyond the Canadian border. It commonly made its home in prairie dog colonies (called towns), taking over part of the tunnel system for its own use as predator in residence. The prairie dogs (burrowing rodents of the squirrel family) made up over 90 percent of the ferret's diet. A single ferret could survive on what it could catch in even quite a small town, but mothers raising families normally took up residence in larger colonies. Mice and other small prey caught outside the burrow at night added to the ferret's prairie dog diet.

Black-footed ferrets do not gather in groups. Instead, they spread themselves out, often living about 3.5 miles (6 km) apart; the low density of animals presumably prevented them from overexploiting their food resources. The ferrets were so dependent on prairie dogs for both food and lodging that when—in the 20th century—prairie dog towns were wiped out wholesale to make way for farmland, the ferrets suffered along with their prey. In Kansas, a former prairie dog stronghold, over 98 percent of the prairie dog population was eliminated in less than 100 years. By the middle of the 20th century the ferrets were feared extinct, although there were reported sightings of individuals from time to time. A small population was even discovered in South Dakota, but the group had apparently died out by 1974.

Back from the Brink

In 1981 a black-footed ferret was killed by dogs on a ranch in Wyoming. Subsequent investigations revealed that a substantial wild population, numbering at least 129 animals, had survived there. The group became the subject of intensive study, but the white-tailed

DATA PANEL

Black-footed ferret

Mustela nigripes

Family: Mustelidae

World population: Probably fewer than 500, mostly in captivity

Distribution: Formerly grasslands of the American Midwest from Texas to the Canadian border; reintroduced into Montana, South Dakota, Arizona, and Wyoming

Habitat: Short-grass prairies; in prairie dog burrows

Size: Length head/body: 15–24 in (49–60 cm); tail: 5–6 in (10–14 cm). Weight: 32–39 oz (915–1,125 g)

Form: Sinuous, short-legged animal, about the size of a small cat; pale yellow in color; black legs, mask, and tail tip

Diet: Mostly small rodents, especially prairie dogs, caught inside the prairie dog burrow. Mice and other small prey caught outside at night

Breeding: One litter per year in March–April; usually 3–4 (but up to 6) young born; young stay with their mothers until early fall. Male offspring may disperse; females often stay near birth site. Life span at least 12 years

Related endangered species: Colombian weasel *(Mustela felipei)* EN; European mink *(M. lutreola)** EN; Indonesian mountain weasel *(M. lutreolina)* EN; black-striped weasel *(M. strigidorsa)* VU

Status: IUCN EW; CITES I

Montana
North Dakota
Wyoming
South Dakota
UNITED STATES
Nebraska
Colorado

See also: Disease **1:** 55; Inbreeding and Interbreeding **1:** 56; Marten, Pine **6:** 74; Prairie Dog, Black-Tailed **7:** 92; Wolverine **10:** 74

prairie dogs on which the ferrets were feeding had suffered a population crash as a result of disease, and the ferrets themselves had been struck down by an outbreak of canine distemper. The last 18 ferrets were taken into captivity as an insurance against total extinction. By 1987 there were no black-footed ferrets left in the wild.

An Uncertain Outlook

In captivity the ferrets' numbers built up slowly, to 70 in 1989 and over 300 by the end of 1991—enough for some to be reintroduced to the wild. Over a period of three years 188 ferrets were released, most of which probably died soon afterward. However, the survivors produced at least six litters of young.

The captive population continued to increase, and by 1996 there were at least 400 animals in various zoos and conservation centers. The United States Fish and Wildlife Service has since carried out new reintroductions, releasing ferrets in Montana, South Dakota, and Arizona.

However, even in protected areas where prairie dogs are no longer trapped, shot, or poisoned, the future for the black-footed ferret looks uncertain. The main problem confronting the species is genetic. The entire surviving population of black-footed ferrets derives from a small handful of animals—the descendants of those taken into captivity in 1987—and as a result is dangerously inbred. Normally such inbreeding leads to poor reproductive success and a reduced chance of survival. It remains to be seen whether the newly restored populations, themselves bred from only a few dozen animals, will overcome their problems and increase to form a viable population. Even if they do, it is unlikely that they will ever again be widespread or numerous, simply because their prairie dog prey has disappeared from most of its former range.

The black-footed ferret *lives in prairie dog burrows. Its underground life and nocturnal habits explain why it is so little known. Yet despite its elusiveness, the ferret leaves tracks that are easily seen in snow, and the animal itself can sometimes be spotted at night by flashlight.*

Finch, Gouldian

Erythrura gouldiae

Once abundant and widespread over much of northern Australia, the beautiful and colorful Gouldian finch is greatly reduced in numbers and breeding sites, due mainly to habitat changes.

Records suggest that in the early 20th century the Gouldian finch was a common and familiar member of its family with an extensive range. During the 20th century, however, the species suffered a dramatic decline both in numbers and distribution. During the 1960s a survey at Pine Creek, Cape York, Australia, caught about 1,000 individuals in one week. A second survey in the same area in 1996 found only half a dozen birds in three months.

It is not surprising that such a stunning-looking bird was popular with cage-bird enthusiasts. Large numbers were caught—legally and illegally—for the Australian and international trade in captive birds until the early 1980s. The numbers of birds legally caught each year by licensed bird trappers were recorded until the end of 1986, when the trapping of Gouldian finches was banned. The statistics showed that between 1972 and 1981 there was an 87 percent decline in numbers caught in Western Australia. At the end of this period—five years before the trapping ban—no Gouldian finches were caught commercially. Large-scale trapping is likely to have depleted populations, but landscape changes are thought to be much more significant.

Gouldian finches are primarily birds of open tropical woodland with a grassy understory, where they are highly selective both in their diet and choice of breeding sites. They feed exclusively on grass seeds; the grass species varies seasonally and geographically. The birds travel over large distances to find supplies to build up their reserves before breeding.

Environmental Change

Gouldian finches are the only members of their family to nest almost exclusively in tree hollows rather than building their own nests. Highly sociable, they breed in loose colonies, preferring clumps of smooth-barked eucalyptus trees, although the species of eucalyptus varies from area to area. At present none of the known breeding sites has long-term protection as a nature reserve.

The Gouldian finch's dependence on a specialized diet makes it sensitive to changes in land management, especially the burning of grasses by farmers. Low-intensity fires

DATA PANEL

Gouldian finch (painted finch, rainbow finch, purple-breasted finch, Lady Gould's finch)

Erythrura gouldiae

Family: Estrildidae

World population: Fewer than 2,500 adults may remain in the wild at the start of the breeding season

Distribution: Northern Australia

Habitat: Dry savanna grassland; fringes of mangroves and thickets; rarely far from water. Woods and scrubland with spinifex grasses in wet season; avoids human habitation

Size: Length: 5–5.5 in (12.5–14 cm). Weight: 0.4–0.5 oz (12–15 g)

Form: Multicolored plumage in adults. Male has green upperparts with circular or oval patch on purple breast; yellow belly and flanks; black tail with long, pointed central feathers. Female duller, with shorter central tail feathers. Juveniles have gray heads and lack bright colors and long tail feathers

Diet: Ripe and part-ripe grass seeds, mainly sorghum in dry season; seeds of other grasses in the wet season

Breeding: Female usually lays 4–8 white eggs directly into tree hollow or termite mound in January–April (rainy season). Incubation 12–13 days; fledging about 21 days

Related endangered species: Green-faced parrotfinch (*Erythrura viridifacies*) VU; Shelley's crimson-wing (*Cryptospiza shelleyi*) VU; Anambra waxbill (*Estrilda poliopareia*) VU; green avadavat (*Amandava formosa*) VU

Status: IUCN EN; not listed by CITES

AUSTRALIA

See also: Specialization **1:** 28; Finch, Mangrove **4:** 76; Honeyeater, Regent **5:** 54

Gouldian finches *come in many color varieties. About 75 percent of birds have black faces and 25 percent have crimson heads; there is also a rare yellow-headed form.*

during the dry season can help the birds find food: Fallen seed is more accessible to the birds after any covering of dead stems and leaves has been burned off. At the end of the dry season, however, intense fires burn off tree leaves, destroying suitable shelter. Fierce fires during the wet season can destroy sorghum grassland, including any emerging seedlings. Food shortages after such fires are often made worse by the fact that cattle graze the affected areas, preventing grasses from seeding. Grazing and the uniform fire regime destroy the mosaic of habitats on which the finches depend. The regular burning destroys clumps of breeding trees, and the birds are known to avoid badly burned tree hollows.

Mite Attack

A symptom of these landscape changes is the high level of infection with a parasitic mite that affects the finch's respiratory system. When birds in captivity are infected, they wheeze and become listless, fail to breed, and die if they are not treated with antibiotics. Although the effects of the mite had not been reported in wild birds, researchers checking for its presence found it occurred in 62 percent of the birds examined. Even though the parasites were not the cause of the massive declines, they may be preventing the species from recovering its numbers.

Recovery Plan

A recovery plan for the Gouldian finch was announced in 1998. Its chief emphasis is an in-depth study of the ecology and habitat needs of the species. The main objective is to stabilize numbers. Initially the numbers and occurrence of the Gouldian finch must be determined. With a small, scarce bird with a huge range this is no easy task, although counts at waterholes have gained useful results so far.

Finch, Mangrove

Camarhynchus heliobates

Confined to its specialized habitat on the isolated Galápagos Islands, the mangrove finch was never widespread. Yet before colonists began destroying its native mangrove forests, it had thrived for millennia. Today the entire population lives in an area no bigger than a shopping mall.

When Charles Darwin visited the Galápagos Islands in 1835, he was struck by the way that every island was inhabited by distinct species of animals, each slightly different from those on neighboring islands. Initially he was drawn to spectacular creatures like the giant tortoises and marine iguanas, but in time he realized that the most significant variations occurred among the 13 species of drab-brown finches scattered throughout the archipelago. The finches all looked a bit alike, yet some had big, sturdy bills for cracking nuts and seeds, while others had smaller bills for feeding on soft fruit and flowers. Yet others had slender bills for catching insects. It became clear to Darwin that the birds were variations on a single evolutionary theme, and his explanation of how this came about was to prove the basis of his revolutionary theory of natural selection.

Darwin's Finches

To this day the Galápagos finches are known as "Darwin's finches." They have a special place in the history of science and are arguably more significant than any carefully preserved historical monument. Yet while most of the finches are still common on the islands, the mangrove finch is in danger of extinction.

Like all the finches on the Galápagos Islands, the mangrove finch has survived—and acquired its identity—by exploiting a particular niche in the island ecosystem. It lives among the mangrove forests that grow in the coastal shallows and around saltwater lagoons, feeding mainly on insects and other small creatures. Historically it was known to inhabit at least six areas of mangrove forest on Isabela Island and nearby Fernandina; but as the mangroves were cut back by the growing human population, so was the area of habitat available to the mangrove finch.

The mangrove finch was last reported on Fernandina in 1971 and is now almost certainly extinct there. Until fairly recently there were viable breeding populations on southeastern Isabela, but surveys in 1997 and 1999 found few birds. The entire known breeding population is now

DATA PANEL

Mangrove finch

Camarhynchus heliobates

Family: Emberizidae

World population: 52 pairs at last count (1999)

Distribution: Two sites in northwestern Isabela, Galápagos Islands, Ecuador

Habitat: Dense mangrove forest

Size: Length: 5.5 in (14 cm). Weight: 0.6 oz (18 g)

Form: Small brown finch with strong, pointed bill. Dull-brown upperparts with olive rump; pale, faintly dark-streaked breast. Male and female alike

Diet: Mainly insects and spiders, plus a small amount of vegetable matter

Breeding: January–May (the rainy season). Male becomes territorial and builds several speculative dome-shaped

nests in the mangroves, displaying to attract a female; after selecting a nest (or helping build a better one) and mating, the female lays 2–5 eggs, incubating them for about 12 days. Some pairs rear more than 1 clutch (up to 5). Chicks fed by both parents and fledge at 13–14 days

Related endangered species: Many species in family Emberizidae, including olive-headed brush finch (*Atlapetes flaviceps*) EN; multicolored tanager (*Chlorochrysa nitidissima*) VU; Guadalupe junco (*Junco insularis*) CR; Cochabamba mountain finch (*Poospiza garleppi*) EN; and Cuban sparrow (*Torreornis inexpectata*) EN

Status: IUCN CR; not listed by CITES

COSTA RICA
PANAMA
COLOMBIA
Galápagos Islands (Ecuador)
ECUADOR
PERU

See also: Categories of Threat **1:** 14; Tanager, Seven-Colored **9:** 54
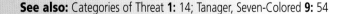

restricted to two adjacent areas of mangrove swamp on the northeastern coast of Isabela, called Playa Tortuga Negra and Caleta Black. Together they cover less than half a square mile.

Mysterious Decline

The mangrove finch may yet flourish within its pitifully small, yet remote stronghold; endangered birds have recovered from worse situations. However, for some reason its numbers are still dwindling. In 1997 there were 21 breeding pairs among the mangroves at Caleta Black, but two years later there were only 16. Meanwhile, the population of 37 pairs at Playa Tortuga Negra had slipped slightly to 36, but even this was a significant loss. Accordingly, the mangrove finch is now classified by the IUCN as Critically Endangered: a species on the edge of oblivion.

The mangrove finch's decline may be as a result of the introduced species that now live on the Galápagos. Among the worst culprits are the black rats that swarm over seven of the islands, including Isabela, eating the eggs and young of native birds. Wild cats are another problem, as is an introduced egg-stealing bird, the smooth-billed ani. Voracious, stinging fire ants have also established colonies on the islands, and anyone who has experienced their ferocity in the southern United States knows how destructive they can be. Another insect invader is a wasp, *Polistes versicolor*, which preys on the insect larvae that form most of the finch's food. Yet none of these is a proven threat to the mangrove finch, and the true reason for its continuing decline remains a mystery.

If the mangrove finch is to survive, we need to know why it is in trouble. Habitat reduction over the 20th century is certainly a factor. However, today the species is strictly protected: the Galápagos have been a World Heritage Site since 1979; and although illegal

The mangrove finch *may occur in unsurveyed areas on Isabela Island, and searching for the species in such places is a high priority.*

activities persist, the remaining mangrove forests on Isabela are in good shape. In an effort to identify why numbers are dwindling, the conservation authorities on the islands—the Galápagos National Park Service and the Charles Darwin Research Center—have initiated research programs to study the finch's breeding biology and to assess the impact of black rat predation. They have also analyzed the birds' blood for evidence of hybridization—a possible reason for the decline—but with no result.

Meanwhile, alien predators and competitors are being controlled, and if linked to careful monitoring of the mangrove finch population, the finch's main enemy may yet be revealed and its future assured.

Firecrown, Juan Fernández

Sephanoides fernandensis

The Juan Fernández firecrown is the flagship species of a remote Pacific island group, a major center of biodiversity. An ambitious conservation program has been launched to save it.

The Juan Fernández firecrown hummingbird is found only in the Juan Fernández archipelago in the southeastern Pacific. Part of the nation of Chile, the island chain consists of two widely separated main islands, Robinson Crusoe Island (or Masatierra) and Alexander Selkirk Island (or Masafuera), and a number of smaller surrounding islets (small islands). They are the exposed peaks of relatively young oceanic volcanoes and were never connected to mainland South America.

The archipelago is one of the world's most important centers of biodiversity, containing many endemic species (those found nowhere else). However, this incredibly rich concentration of wildlife has been threatened and impoverished by over 400 years of clearance and degradation of native vegetation by settlers and the animals they brought with them—overgrazing has affected the islands' remarkable flora since 1574. Some areas have been denuded of native vegetation, while others have been overrun by nonnative species. Today only about 10 percent of the original native forest remains intact.

A Perilous Situation

The remaining population of the Juan Fernández firecrown is estimated to be only a few hundred birds. Records suggest that the species was once far more abundant, possibly numbering 20,000 birds in the 19th century. Although it occurred on both the main islands, it has gone from Alexander Selkirk Island. The birds there belonged to the race *leyboldi,* but none has been recorded since 1908, and this distinct subspecies is regarded as extinct. On Robinson Crusoe Island birds of the race *fernandensis* are mainly confined to an area of remnant native forest around the island's main settlement, San Juan Bautista.

The reasons for the firecrown's disappearance from Alexander Selkirk Island and its current small numbers are complex. It would appear that overgrazing and habitat alteration are the major causes, limiting the availability, quantity, and quality of the bird's food. The species feeds on nectar from various native flowers, but has adapted to feed from introduced species of eucalyptus and flowers,

---

DATA PANEL

Juan Fernández firecrown

Sephanoides fernandensis

Family: Trochilidae

World population: 200–400 birds

Distribution: Restricted area of Robinson Crusoe Island in Juan Fernández archipelago west of mainland Chile in Pacific Ocean

Habitat: Remnant native forest and cultivated areas, including gardens

Size: Length: male 4.8 in (12 cm); female 4 in (10.5 cm). Weight: male 0.4 oz (11 g); female 0.25 oz (7 g)

Form: Male cinnamon-orange with iridescent brilliant red-yellow forehead and crown, wings copper-gray. Female iridescent purple-blue crown, blue-green upperparts; white underparts decorated with green and black spots and black-green wings

Diet: Mainly nectar from native species, but also introduced plants; some insects from leaves or in flight

Breeding: Details not known. The few nests recorded are small and well above ground, among cover; one was made of finely woven fibers of ferns

Related endangered species: Include the sapphire-bellied hummingbird (*Lepidopyga lilliae*) CR; Bogotá sunangel (*Heliangelus zusii*) CR; colorful puffleg (*Eriocnemis mirabilis*) CR; Chilean woodstar (*Eulidia yarrellii*) EN; marvelous spatuletail (*Loddigesia mirabilis*)* EN; violet-throated metaltail (*Metallura baroni*) EN; Perijá metaltail (*M. iracunda*) VU; little woodstar (*Acestrura bombus*) VU; purple-backed sunbeam (*Aglaeactis aliciae*) VU; bee hummingbird (*Mellisuga helenae*)* LRnt

Status: IUCN CR; CITES II

CHILE

Juan Fernández Islands (Chile)
Alexander-Selkirk ■ Robinson Crusoe

ARGENTINA

See also: Archipelagos 1: 32; Introductions 1: 54; Saving the Habitats 1: 88; Hummingbird, Bee 5: 62; Spatuletail, Marvelous 9: 20

particularly during the southern fall and winter, when only one native flowering plant is in bloom.

Other factors contributing to the firecrown's perilous position are introduced predators, notably cats, rats, and coatis. A threat may also be posed by its close relative, the green-backed firecrown. Widespread in mainland Chile south of the Atacama Desert, this species is—or was—found on both the Juan Fernández main islands. A natural colonizer, it probably became isolated from its cousin between half a million and a million years ago. It has been abundant on Robinson Crusoe Island only since the late 19th century. The population in the late 1980s was estimated at between 4,000 and 6,000. It was first observed on Alexander Selkirk Island in 1981, where it was said to be widespread, although none has been seen there recently.

The sexes of the green-backed firecrown are very similar, differing only slightly in size, while those of the Juan Fernández firecrown are very different; they were

The Juan Fernández firecrown *is a vibrant, beautiful hummingbird that faces an uncertain future.*

originally classified as separate species in the 19th century. The female Juan Fernández firecrown is about 66 percent smaller than the male. Researchers think that while males can defend prime territories, the females may be outcompeted by the larger green-backed firecrown; the sex ratio in Juan Fernández firecrowns is three males to each female.

Urgent Requirements

Although designated as a national park as long ago as 1935, the islands have been protected only since 1967. They were recently nominated a World Heritage site. The Chilean government has embarked on an ambitious conservation program that aims to restore habitat and native vegetation and to control introduced species. Unless such measures succeed, this bird is probably doomed.

Flamingo, Andean

Phoenicoparrus andinus

The rarest of the world's five species of flamingos, the Andean flamingo lives in a few remote high mountain lakes of the Andes Mountains. Its survival is threatened by the continuing exploitation and deterioration of its habitat.

The Andean flamingo belongs to one of the oldest of all bird families, which originated over 50 million years ago. Today they are found on the puna—a high, cold, dry plateau in the Andes Mountains, usually at heights of between 7,500 and 14,750 feet (2,300 and 4,500 m). They live in lakes, where they wade in water 10 times as salty as the sea.

Although the lakes appear to be inhospitable, they are productive habitats, containing huge concentrations of diatoms, or microscopic single-cell algae (plants that have no true stems, roots, and leaves) on which the flamingos feed. The bizarre-looking bills of Andean flamingos are specially adapted for feeding in shallow water. The birds dunk their heads in the water, holding the bill upside down. The bill contains rows of comblike structures with which the birds sieve out the tiny food items by pumping water through the bill with a pistonlike action of the large tongue.

Multiple Threats

Only one species of flamingo, the greater flamingo, is not considered threatened. The other four, even with a combined population of several million birds, are considered at risk from hunting, because of a long breeding cycle, and because there are fewer than 30 major breeding sites in the world. The situation for the Andean flamingo is particularly serious: It has the smallest population, which has recently shown a serious decline—equal to 24 percent in the 15 years since the mid-1980s. Breeding success is consistently low; and since the adults are long-lived (up to 50 years), numbers are unlikely to recover for many years.

The species nests at only 10 or so major colonies; and despite their remoteness, the breeding sites are coming under increasing pressure. Away from the protected colonies the flamingos are still regularly hunted (on a small scale) for their meat, feathers, and fat, which is used in traditional medicine and considered to be a cure for tuberculosis in some parts of the Andes. Most of the birds killed are juveniles.

A more serious threat is posed by the removal of eggs by local people, especially if they are sold in quantity rather than being used for personal consumption. The problem was especially acute during the 1950s to the early 1980s, when many eggs were taken from nests each year.

80

See also: Specialization 1: 28; Stork, Greater Adjutant 9: 34

Both an increase in mining activities near breeding colonies and the towns that service the mining developments pose major threats to the flamingo's habitat. Along with the problem of water pollution, increased disturbance at the colonies from human activity can cause breeding failure. The diversion of streams for mining operations and other uses or changes in weather also result in fluctuating water levels. Such factors can cause droughts and consequently a lack of food or destruction of nests by flooding.

Surveys of the high-altitude salt and alkaline lakes of the Andes have revealed the species' status and population trends and located new colonies. A priority in the future is to maintain habitat, halt deterioration, and prevent hunting and egg-collecting by protecting more breeding sites. Four sites currently receive official protection to some degree.

The Andean flamingo is endangered for many reasons, but low breeding success is a critical factor.

DATA PANEL

Andean flamingo

Phoenicoparrus andinus

Family: Phoenicopteridae

World population: Fewer than 34,000 birds

Distribution: The high Andean plateaus of Peru, Argentina, Bolivia, and Chile

Habitat: High mountain alkaline and salt lakes

Size: Length: 39–42 in (99–110 cm)

Form: Large waterbird with long neck and long legs. Downward-bent bill, pale yellow at the base, black on the downcurved portion. Plumage pale pink with bright upperparts and deep wine-red tinge to head, neck, upper breast, and wing coverts (small feathers covering the base of the flight feathers). Primary flight feathers of wingtips form a large black triangular patch when the wings are closed. Young birds are gray with heavily streaked upperparts

Diet: Diatoms (microscopic single-cell algae)

Breeding: Breeds in large social colonies of birds (including other species). Female lays 1 white egg in shallow pit atop a nest of mud. Incubation period about 4 weeks; chicks have pale-gray down and are at first fed on a milklike secretion from the adults' upper digestive tract; they fledge at 10–12 weeks; acquire adult plumage at 3 years

Related endangered species: Chilean flamingo (*Phoenicopterus chilensis*) LRnt; lesser flamingo (*P. minor*) LRnt; puna flamingo (*Phoenicoparrus jamesi*) LRnt

Status: IUCN VU; CITES II

Flycatcher, Pacific Royal

Onychorhynchus occidentalis

An unusual member of one of the most successful and diverse of all bird families, the royal flycatcher is increasingly suffering from the destruction of its tropical forest home in South America. It is now reduced to a few fragmented areas of its former range.

There are some 420 species in the New World family of tyrant flycatchers, and in general they are an extremely successful group of birds. They have adapted to many different habitats and lifestyles throughout the Americas, and many of them are common and widespread birds.

Sadly, this is not the case with the Pacific royal flycatcher, one of the most spectacular of all the members of this bird family and also one of the most threatened. In common with most of its relatives, it is small and drably plumaged, and like many other species of tyrant-flycatchers, it has a patch of usually concealed brightly colored feathers on top of its head. Unlike other species, however, this is literally the royal flycatcher's crowning glory. When sufficiently aroused

Pacific royal flycatchers *display a magnificently colored fan at times of mating, competition, or preening. With their long bill-bristles and short legs, they are distinctive birds.*

during courtship, a competitive encounter with a rival, or perhaps when preening in the rain, the bird puts up its crest, forming a spectacularly colorful, semicircular fan that spreads across the head.

Another feature distinguishing the bird from its relatives is that while many of them have modified feathers known as rictal bristles around the base of the bill, those of the Pacific royal flycatcher are exceptionally long—almost as long as the bill itself—as well as being markedly flattened from top to bottom. The broad shape of the bill helps the birds catch butterflies and other insects in flight, while the long bristles may help funnel the prey into the mouth and

DATA PANEL

Pacific royal flycatcher (royal flycatcher)

Onychorhynchus occidentalis

Family: Tyrannidae

World population: 2,500–10,000 birds

Distribution: Western Ecuador, from Esmeraldas Province south to El Oro Province, including the adjoining part of the Tumbes Department in northwestern Peru

Habitat: Humid and deciduous lowland forests below 3,900 ft (1,200 m); has been recorded in degraded forest

Size: Length: 6.3–6.5 in (16–16.5 cm). Weight: about 0.8 oz (21 g)

Form: Sparrow-sized bird with long, broad bill fringed with long bristles; large crest normally held flat gives head hammerhead shape: occasionally erected to form a crosswise, brightly colored fan. Both sexes have drab upperparts, unmarked apart from small buff spots on wing-coverts, chestnut rump, and tail; whitish throat; rest of underparts orange-buff, brightest on breast. In the male the fan is mostly shiny scarlet with scattered black spots and feathers tipped with blue; in the female scarlet is replaced by paler orange-yellow

Diet: Mainly large insects such as butterflies, bugs, and dragonflies caught in flight or in darting sallies from branch to branch

Breeding: Nest is a long, slender structure of plant fibers, rootlets, dry leaves, live epiphytes (plants that grow on other plants), and small amounts of moss suspended from a hanging vine or drooping branch high above a shaded stream, sheltered from wind; lays 2 deep reddish-brown eggs

Related endangered species: Atlantic royal flycatcher *(Onychorhynchus swainsoni)* EN

Status: IUCN VU; not listed by CITES

82

See also: Pasture **1:** 38; National Parks **1:** 92; Dipper, Rufous-Throated **4:** 18; Siskin, Red **8:** 94

protect the eyes against damage. Even when closed, the elongated feathers of the crest—although much less conspicuous—project behind the bird's head, sometimes showing a little of their color. Together with the long bill, this gives the Pacific royal flycatcher an odd, hammerheaded appearance. Another distinguishing feature is the shortness of its legs compared with other tyrant flycatchers.

For most of the time the flycatcher remains inconspicuous, searching for food unobtrusively in the shade of the low to middle levels of the forest, often in mixed-species flocks, but also alone or in pairs.

Lowland Forest Destruction

The Pacific royal flycatcher has been recorded within a few areas of western Ecuador and adjacent northwestern Peru in isolated patches of humid and deciduous lowland forest at altitudes from sea level to 3,900 feet (1,200 m). The fact that there are records from degraded forest suggests that it may be able to

feed in such places but still needs unmodified, moister forest during the breeding season. Across its range it is apparently scarce and localized, and in most places it seems to be on the brink of extinction.

A major problem facing the Pacific royal flycatcher is that it occurs exclusively in lowland forest, much of which below an altitude of 2,900 feet (900 m) has already been felled for timber; logging even threatens protected areas such as Ecuador's Cordillera de Molleturo Protection Forest. The subsequent human settlement in many areas brings intensive grazing by goats and cattle, which prevents trees from regenerating and, more importantly, clears the understory of remaining forest. This also applies to some protected areas in both Ecuador and Peru.

If the destruction of the Pacific royal flycatcher's habitat continues or increases, its status may need to be revised to Endangered. There is an urgent need to prevent further habitat loss and to establish new, more effectively protected areas.

Flying Fox, Rodrigues

Pteropus rodricensis

Limited in numbers and confined to a single island, the Rodrigues flying fox—a bat—is threatened by habitat loss, starvation, and the periodic devastation caused by cyclones.

The flying foxes—so called because of their foxlike faces, complete with pointed muzzles—form a group of about 60 species of large fruit bat inhabiting the islands and coastal states of the Indo-Pacific region. Unlike the smaller bat species, which navigate primarily by echolocation (a system for determining the position of objects using echoes), flying foxes rely on keen senses of sight and smell to find their way around. Several species of flying fox are now severely endangered, none more so than the Rodrigues flying fox. This bat is confined to the island of Rodrigues, one of the Mascarene group, of which Mauritius is the largest.

The islands lie far out in the Indian Ocean, so no nonflying mammals have managed to colonize them naturally. The bats living on the islands have evolved to form endemic species (ones found nowhere else in the world). The closely related greater Mascarene flying fox lives on Mauritius. While it is classified by the IUCN as Vulnerable, the Rodrigues bat is now considered highly endangered because of its low numbers and the limited habitat available to it.

A Story of Declining Numbers

The bats have been in decline for nearly 100 years, but were still fairly common early in the 20th century. As late as 1955 there were several colonies in different parts of Rodrigues Island, totaling about 1,000 bats. Ten years later several hundred could still be found, but by the 1970s only a few dozen remained. Like other fruit bats, the Rodrigues flying fox has been hunted for food in the past, although it is now given full legal protection.

More significantly, the bat depends on a sequence of fruits ripening at different times throughout the year to provide it with food. When the mixed forests in which it lives are cut down and replaced with single-species plantations, the pattern is disrupted, so there may be no food available during some seasons. Forest clearance also reduces the total number of fruiting trees, imposing a limit on the population the island can support. In the late 1950s a large group of tamarind trees was cut down on Rodrigues, despite the fact that tamarind pods are a favorite food for the bat.

The small size of the island, which covers only 42 square miles (110 sq. km), must always have limited the flying foxes' numbers, but human-induced changes have exerted great pressure on the

---

DATA PANEL

Rodrigues flying fox

Pteropus rodricensis

Family: Pteropodidae

World population: 1,500–2,000

Distribution: Rodrigues Island, off Mauritius, Indian Ocean

Habitat: Dry, mixed palm tree woodland

Size: Length: 6 in (15 cm); wingspan: 36 in (90 cm). Weight: 12–13 oz (350 g)

Form: Dark-brown bat, often with paler head and shoulders; black wings

Diet: Mostly fruit; also leaves, pollen, and flowers

Breeding: One young born per year, usually in August–December. Young stay with mother for 1 year. Life span probably more than 15 years

Related endangered species: Ryukyu flying fox *(Pteropus dasymallus)** EN. The IUCN lists 34 other species of *Pteropus*, including 5 that are Critically Endangered

Status: IUCN CR; CITES II

COMOROS

MADAGASCAR

MAURITIUS

Rodrigues

Réunion (France)

See also: Island Biogeography **1:** 30; Flying Fox, Ryukyu **4:** 86

bat. A particular problem for the bats, in addition to the difficulties caused by people, is the natural threat posed by cyclones. Periodically, mighty winds tear through the island and devastate the bats' habitat. Trees are ripped up, and leaves and fruits are torn from the branches. The bats are not strong fliers, and any that are carried away are inevitably blown out to sea, where they drown. Those that do survive the tempest face a time of hunger, since few fruits are left on the trees, and it can be months before others ripen to replace the lost crop.

When a disaster of this kind hits an already small population, sudden extinction becomes a real possibility. By 1978 there were only about 200 flying foxes left on Rodrigues. The following year Cyclone Celine II struck, reducing the population to just 70, and making the Rodrigues flying fox the world's rarest bat overnight.

Over the next 10 years numbers built up again to about 1,000. Yet another cyclone hit the island in 1991, cutting the bat population by two-thirds. Reduced numbers also mean a loss of genetic diversity, a problem that has repeatedly afflicted the species and that may reduce its viability in the long term.

In Captivity

Fortunately, 18 bats were taken into captivity in 1976 to form breeding colonies in Mauritius and at the Jersey Wildlife Preservation Trust in Britain. The bats have bred well, and at least nine zoos, including some in the United States, now have specimens in their collections. As a result, there are currently several hundred Rodrigues flying foxes in captivity—enough to support a controlled release onto an Indian Ocean island outside the cyclone belt. Such a step would mean introducing the species to an environment in which it is not native—always risky, since the effect of

The Rodrigues flying fox *is now given full legal protection. It plays an important ecological role in pollinating forest trees and helping disperse their seeds.*

introduced animals on the other native flora and fauna cannot be predicted. Yet without such a safety net there will be the risk that a single severe storm could wipe out the Rodrigues flying fox in the wild.

85

Flying Fox, Ryukyu

Pteropus dasymallus

The Ryukyu flying fox is typical of many fruit bats living on islands; it faces a range of threats, and already one subspecies seems to be extinct.

There are five local varieties of the Ryukyu flying fox, which vary in size and color. They each live on different islands; and because their habitats are mostly small, the animals have probably never been very numerous.

The flying foxes are not foxes at all, but large fruit-eating bats. They live in the warmer regions of Asia and on islands in the Pacific and Indian Oceans. Like other flying foxes, they form colonies, hanging like furled umbrellas, spaced out along the bare branches of trees. Sometimes the colonies are large and conspicuous. Their habit of hanging out in the open makes the bats vulnerable to the slightest disturbance and to being shot or captured.

Capture is a common problem for all the larger fruit bats, since they are meaty and good to eat. Large numbers have been routinely collected for food, often by plundering the nursery colonies where the young bats are reared. Such disturbance results in the loss or abandonment of many youngsters. Like other bats, if the young fall to the ground before they can fly properly, they are generally unable to get airborne again. Often they are killed by dogs, land crabs, and even armies of ants. Bats also produce only one young a year, so replacement of losses is a slow process.

Ecological Eating

Fruit bats feed mainly on soft fruit borne by trees in the forest. They often just squeeze the fruit in their mouths and swallow only the juice, spitting out (or dropping) most of the pips and pulp at some distance from the tree. Any swallowed pips or seeds pass undamaged through the digestive tract and are discarded with the feces, often miles from where the fruit was collected. This is an important mechanism for dispersing the seeds of forest trees. Many fruit bats, including the Ryukyu flying fox, also feed on flowers at certain times of the year and help pollinate them, thus performing another essential ecological role. Consequently, the preservation of fruit bat populations is needed for the continued survival of a sustainable forest ecosystem.

DATA PANEL

Ryukyu flying fox	**Size:** Length: 8 in (22 cm); wingspan: over 3 ft (1 m). Weight: 1 lb (400–450 g)	**Breeding:** One young born per year. Life span unknown but could be 20 years
Pteropus dasymallus	**Form:** Large fruit bat with typical "foxy" face and big eyes. Varies in color from pale brown to black, sometimes with pale collar or chest	**Related endangered species:** Rodrigues flying fox *(Pteropus rodricensis)** CR. The IUCN lists 34 other species of *Pteropus* among the threatened mammals, including 5 that are Critically Endangered
Family: Pteropodidae	**Diet:** Variety of fruit, especially figs; also flowers, insects, and leaves	
World population: A few hundred		**Status:** IUCN EN; CITES II
Distribution: Ryukyu (Nansei) Islands, Japan		
Habitat: Forest, fruit trees		

NORTH KOREA
SOUTH KOREA
JAPAN
CHINA
Ryukyu Islands
TAIWAN

See also: Communities and Ecosystems **1:** 22; Flying Fox, Rodrigues **4:** 84

A Fragile Future

The conservation of flying foxes and other fruit bats is essential, yet many species are threatened and fast disappearing. For example, numbers of the Taiwanese subspecies of the Ryukyu flying fox have declined sharply as a result of poor enforcement of protection laws. Recent surveys have failed to find any individuals, and this flying fox may already be extinct. Elsewhere, other subspecies of the Ryukyu flying fox are threatened by loss of habitat in which to roost and feed as trees are removed for the timber industry, fuel, and to create farmland.

In the past hunters have killed large numbers of flying foxes, reducing the population drastically. In some places the bats also sustain losses through flying

The Ryukyu flying fox, *like other species of flying fox, has a doglike face and large ears. Flying foxes navigate using their eyesight and sense of smell to locate the fruit and flowers on which they feed at night.*

into overhead electricity and telephone wires. Contact with the wires can result in electrocution, strangulation, or broken wings.

The Japanese government has given the Ryukyu flying fox legal protection. However, it has not created any protected areas in which the bats can live undisturbed. Although the flying fox is reported to be numerous on a couple of the islands around Japan, forest removal is still badly affecting the Ryukyu group.

Fody, Mauritius

Foudia rubra

One of six species of weaverbirds found on various islands in the Indian Ocean, the colorful Mauritius fody is the rarest due to habitat clearance and the effects of introduced predators.

As its name suggests, the home of this attractive little bird is the island of Mauritius, in the Indian Ocean. Just over half the size of the United States' smallest state, Rhode Island, Mauritius has been an independent country since 1968, together with Rodrigues, another of the Mascarene Islands. The forests have been replaced over hundreds of years by plantations of sugar cane, tea, and alien conifers. Today only about 5 percent of the original forest cover remains, chiefly in the southwest of the island around the Black River Gorge.

As a result of the effects of humans, including hunting and other forms of direct exploitation in some cases, Mauritius has already lost a number of its endemic bird species, including the famous dodo and the Mauritius blue pigeon, as well as two species of parrot, an owl, a duck, a goose, and a night-heron. Today all the endemic birds are threatened because of habitat destruction and degradation and the introduction of various mammals and birds that prey on the birds' eggs and young.

Forest Destruction

A major cause of the fody's present plight is the massive clearance of native upland forest on Mauritius. Even in the small areas of remaining forest in the Black River Gorge region, introduced animals—from deer, pigs, monkeys, and rats to giant African snails and many different insects—and a range of introduced plants destroy or compete with the native species. Another factor in the destruction of the native vegetation is the frequent occurrence of cyclones (tropical storms) that are very damaging to already degraded areas of forest. They also cause direct damage by destroying nests, eggs, and chicks.

Alien Enemies and Competitors

As with so many other threatened birds, it is not just the destruction of habitat by humans and the animals they have introduced that has put the Mauritius fody in peril, but also the direct effects of predation by some of the newcomers. The most damaging of these alien invaders have been two mammal predators: the crab-eating macaque (a monkey) and the black rat. Between them their plundering of the fodies' eggs

---

DATA PANEL

Mauritius fody

Foudia rubra

Family: Ploceidae

World population: 210–250 birds

Distribution: Found only in part of southwestern Mauritius

Habitat: Native forests, including those dominated by pines and degraded forest invaded by nonnative trees

Size: Length: 5.5 in (14 cm)

Form: Bird slightly smaller than a sparrow; large head, thick neck, plump body, and short tail; male has bright red head, neck, and breast with a small black patch between the eye and the bill; back, wings, and tail dark brown, streaked with buff; reddish rump and uppertail coverts (feathers covering base of upper tail). Female much duller, mainly drab dark brown. Male molts into a femalelike plumage

for a very short period in winter. Juvenile similar to female

Diet: Mainly insects; also some fruit and nectar

Breeding: Nest of dried leaves, mosses, and plant fibers, well-lined with soft feathers and usually sited at the end of a branch; built mainly by the male; 3 pale blue eggs incubated for about 14 days; young fledge in about 18–20 days

Related endangered species: Thirteen other species in the weaverbird family are threatened, including 2 other species of fody: the Seychelles fody *(Foudia sechellarum)* VU and Rodrigues fody *(F. flavicans)* VU

Status: IUCN CR; not listed by CITES

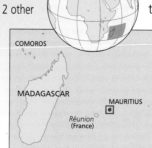

COMOROS

MADAGASCAR

MAURITIUS

Réunion
(France)

See also: Island Biogeography **1:** 30; Captive Breeding **1:** 87; Finch, Mangrove **4:** 76; Lark, Raso **6:** 18

**The male
Mauritius
fody** *has a
striking bright
red head, neck,
and breast.*

and young have led to an almost total failure of the birds to breed in most parts of their range. Two species of mongoose (the small Indian mongoose and the Indian gray mongoose), both introduced to Mauritius in an attempt to prevent the black rats from damaging the sugar-cane plantations, have also been implicated in predation on Mauritius fodies.

Another possible threat comes from a very close relative, the Madagascar fody, which was introduced to Mauritius (and other Indian Ocean islands) during the 19th century. Today it is common throughout the island and may compete for resources with the native fody on Mauritius: That is the case with another threatened fody species on the island of Rodrigues. Unlike the Madagascan fody, the Mauritius fody breeds only once a year (in early summer) and is a more specialized feeder that may be less able to adapt to degraded habitats.

Rescue Program

Known locally as the cardinal, the Mauritius fody is reputed to bring luck if it enters the home. Today this little bird needs all the luck it can get—as well as the help of dedicated and informed conservationists—if it is to survive into the future.

The species is classified as Critically Endangered because its now tiny population is suffering a rapid decline that has been going on for the past 26 years.

Since 1993 there has been a slowing of the rate of decline, together with an increase in range in the main breeding subpopulation. Another tiny subpopulation (only four pairs) has stayed at the same level, but in another very small subpopulation (seven pairs) the decline in both range and population has continued.

Attempts to reverse the overall decline include the setting up of a captive-breeding program and the control of macaques and black rats as part of a plan to restore areas of native vegetation. Aims include the setting up of a Conservation Management Area where predators are strictly controlled, and nectar-producing plants are introduced to supply the fodies with food. Captive-bred birds could be introduced to increase numbers in Mauritius, and new populations could be established on offshore islets (small islands) once these areas have had their native vegetation restored and introduced predators have been eradicated.

Fossa

Cryptoprocta ferox

The catlike fossa of Madagascar is actually more closely related to a mongoose than a cat. The diverse forests in which it lives are shrinking fast, and its future looks uncertain.

The island of Madagascar off the east coast of Africa is nature's own genetics laboratory. Isolated from the African mainland for over 65 million years, the animals and plants of Madagascar have evolved in quite unique ways. The island is home to a large number of species that are found nowhere else in the world. One such animal is the fossa, the island's largest native predator.

The fossa was once thought to be a primitive species of cat. In fact, it belongs to the Viverridae, a family of small- to medium-sized carnivorous mammals that also includes mongoose and the catlike civets and genets of Africa, southern Europe, and Asia. On Madagascar the fossa is related to the fanaloka and the falanouc, which are now very rare. The fossa is larger than most of its cousins, its legs are not as short, and its head is especially catlike, with a short jaw, large, forward-facing eyes, and large, rounded ears. In the absence of any other large, arboreal carnivore on Madagascar the fossa has evolved to fill much the same niche as that occupied by the clouded leopard in Asia.

Life in the Trees

The fossa is a highly skilled climber and spends most of its life in and among trees. Like a cat, it can retract its claws when they are not in use. Most of the fossa's close relatives trot along on their toes, but the fossa uses the whole of its foot to walk on. This stance and gait (described as plantigrade) mean that the fossa's movements are like those of a small, lithe bear.

Fossas sleep by day and hunt at night. Their short, powerful legs and stout, curved claws are ideal for scaling trunks and branches. They are also well adapted to tracking prey since their senses of sight, smell, and hearing are excellent. Fossas will eat just about anything they can catch, including insects, birds, frogs, and small mammals such as tenrecs—members of the Madagascan family Tenrecidae that resemble hedgehogs and shrews. The animal will even pursue nimble lemurs through the branches. Prey is usually trapped with a foot and killed with a quick bite to the

DATA PANEL

Fossa

Cryptoprocta ferox

Family: Viverridae

World population: Unknown; perhaps only a few hundred

Distribution: Island of Madagascar, excluding central highlands

Habitat: Savanna and forest

Size: Length head/body: 24–32 in (60–80 cm); tail: 22 in (65 cm); height at shoulder: 15 in (37 cm); males slightly larger than females. Weight: 15–44 lb (7–20 kg)

Form: Catlike with short, red-brown fur and long, cylindrical tail; small head with large, forward-facing eyes, short jaws, and large, rounded ears. The feet are webbed with retractile claws. The female genitalia look like those of the male

Diet: Small mammals, birds, reptiles, amphibians, and insects

Breeding: Breeds at 4 years of age; 2–4 young born December–January. Life span up to 20 years in captivity

Related endangered species: Falanouc (*Eupleres goudotii*) EN; fanaloka (*Fossa fossana*) VU

Status: IUCN EN; CITES II

90

See also: Speciation 1: 26; Island Biogeography 1: 30; Habitat Loss 1: 38; Bear, Spectacled 2: 74

neck. The fossa has fewer teeth than other viverrids, but those it has are sharp and effective!

Fossa territories usually cover about 0.4 square miles (1 sq. km), and the resident fossa will mark out its boundaries with scent from a large gland at the base of its tail. Fossas do not generally fight over territory, and aggression is more likely during the breeding season. Rivals make threatening calls and postures at each other before launching an all-out attack.

Fossas mate in September and October. The females have a three-month gestation and give birth in a den, either in a tree or a secure spot at ground level. The young are very small, weighing about 3 ounces (100 g) each. The babies are fully furred at birth, but it may be as long as three and a half weeks before they open their eyes. They feed entirely on milk for the first three months, then begin to eat meat. The weaning process takes about six weeks, after which the youngsters follow their mother out of the den at night when she goes hunting. They stay with her for between 15 and 20 months before finding a territory of their own. By this time they are fully grown but will not breed until they are four years old.

Obstacles to Survival

The fossa prefers to live at low population densities and requires large areas of undisturbed forest. Like other Madagascan species, the animal is at risk because of the continuing encroachment by humans on its habitat. Huge areas of savanna and forest have been destroyed, and more is being lost all the time. The fossa is also widely hunted by the Malagasy people.

The fossa *hunts, sleeps, and even raises its young in the trees.*

Fox, Swift

Vulpes velox

The small swift fox has suffered heavy losses as a result of trapping and poisoning campaigns intended to eradicate other more abundant carnivores that were thought to be a threat to livestock.

The swift fox is sometimes regarded as a North American subspecies of the common kit fox. However, the two have a different distribution, and the distinctive DNA and skeletal structures of the swift fox justify treating it as a separate species.

Swift foxes live in small family groups, occupying underground dens with an extensive system of burrows and chambers. The tunnels provide cool shelter during the heat of the day and hiding places in open habitats. For these reasons the burrows are also attractive to rodents and other small animals such as lizards and beetles, which also occupy the dens, providing the foxes with some extra food.

Threats to Survival

Swift foxes are found in open prairie and desert habitats. They used to occur from Canada in the north to the Mexican border in the south. However, in the more northerly states much of their habitat has been taken over as farmland. Swift foxes are relatively tame, and this has contributed to their decline. They are easily trapped, and many were caught for their fur; others have been shot or killed by road traffic. Swift foxes also fall prey to the coyote, a larger relative that is the main predator of the swift foxes' cubs.

Swift foxes are nocturnal hunters. They feed mainly on rabbits and small mammals, and in so doing probably help farmers by destroying pests such as rats and mice. In addition, they do not harm chickens or other livestock. Despite this, the severe decline of swift fox numbers has been caused by their becoming unwitting victims of poisoning campaigns. Poisons directed at coyotes and other predators that are more abundant and perceived as a threat to farm livestock have been picked up by the foxes. In many areas state and local governments have actively encouraged large-scale poisoning campaigns aimed at reducing the numbers of coyotes. As a result, swift foxes became extinct in Canada and are now also very rare in the northern United States.

Reintroduction into Canada

Attempts to reintroduce the swift fox into Canada began in the early 1980s. From 1983 to 1997 a total of 91 wild foxes were caught and taken to Canada for release. They were joined by 841 more that had been raised in captivity. Seventeen sites were selected for the release of foxes in Alberta and south-central Saskatchewan. Initially the foxes were studied carefully after release and were provided with shelters, but after 1987 they were simply turned loose. The captive-bred animals seemed to cope well with freedom, even though most had never been outside a cage.

In 1988 over 30 pups were reared in the wild, but it is still not clear whether the species will become fully established again in Canada. Despite hundreds being released, in 1997 the total Canadian population was still fewer than 200. The project has been criticized, since none of the animals were of Canadian stock, all coming from farther south. Moreover, swift foxes seem to have been slowly spreading northward on their own, suggesting that there was no need for human intervention and that recolonization of suitable areas will eventually take place naturally.

The swift fox *is similar in appearance to the common red fox, but is much smaller. Along with the kit fox, it is the smallest member of the dog family in North America.*

See also: Reintroduction **1:** 92; Dog, Bush **4:** 24; Wolf, Red **10:** 72

Swift fox

Vulpes velox

Family: Canidae

World population: Low thousands

Distribution: Confined to western U.S.; was extinct in Canada but has been reintroduced

Habitat: Open plains and deserts

Size: Length head/body: 15–20 in (36–48 cm); tail: 9–12 in (22–30 cm). Weight: 4–6 lb (1.8–2.7 kg)

Form: Small, large-eared, buff-yellow fox with black markings on either side of muzzle and bushy tail with black tip

Diet: Small mammals; occasionally large insects

Breeding: Between 4 and 7 pups born February–April. Life span up to 7 years in the wild, 20 years in captivity

Related endangered species: Falkland Island wolf *(Dusicyon australis)** EX; red wolf *(Canis rufus)** CR; Ethiopian wolf *(C. simensis)** CR; African wild dog *(Lycaon pictus)** EN; bushdog *(Speothos venaticus)* VU; dhole *(Cuon alpinus)** VU

Status: IUCN LRcd; not listed by CITES

Frog, Gastric-Brooding

Rheobatrachus silus

Notable for the unique mode of reproduction by which they are named, the gastric-brooding frogs of Queensland were never common. Now they may have been wiped out by a disease that has affected many frogs in Australia.

With the probable extinction of its two species of gastric-brooding frog, Australia —and the world—have lost animals with a unique form of reproduction. Found only in a small area of Queensland, the gastric-brooding frog was not discovered until 1973. It has not been seen since 1981, despite several intensive searches being made. The decline in its population was particularly dramatic during 1979. The frog's close relative, the northern gastric-brooding frog, which was not discovered until 1984, also suffered a catastrophic population decline in the following year.

Little is known about the gastric-brooding frog's behavior; mating has never been observed, for example. However, its breeding patterns are unique. Most species of frog lay eggs in water or on moist ground, or they develop inside one of the parents. Fertilization is mostly external, and the eggs generally pass through a free-swimming tadpole stage. Sometimes, however, the tadpoles are immobile and develop directly into tiny froglets. In the gastric-brooding frog females are known to lay between 26 and 40 eggs. However, at some stage in their development, either as eggs or as tadpoles, the female swallows some or all of her offspring, which then develop in her stomach. The process of swallowing the young has never been seen. After six or seven weeks the female delivers between six and 25 fully developed but tiny froglets through her mouth.

Some aspects of the frog's extraordinary reproductive system were studied in the laboratory by a scientist called Michael Tyler. He reasoned that for the mode of reproduction to work, there must be a mechanism by which the young are not digested by their mother's gastric juices. Tyler found that the developing larvae secrete prostaglandin, a hormonelike chemical that inhibits (prevents) the production of digestive acid by the mother's stomach. The chemical is also thought to inhibit peristalsis—the involuntary muscular contractions that move food along the alimentary tract during digestion.

Hidden Habitat

Confined to the Conondale and Blackall mountain ranges in southeastern Queensland, the gastric-brooding frog is well adapted to its aquatic way of life. The toes of the hind feet are fully webbed,

DATA PANEL

Gastric-brooding frog (platypus frog)

Rheobatrachus silus

Family: Myobatrachidae

World population: Probably 0

Distribution: Southeastern Queensland, Australia

Habitat: Rocky mountain creeks

Size: Length: male 1.3–1.6 in (3.3–4.1 cm); female 1.8–2.2 in (4.5–5.4 cm)

Form: Small frog with blunt snout, large eyes, long fingers and toes, and webbed hind feet. Brown or black on back; white on belly; yellow on limbs

Diet: Small invertebrates

Breeding: In summer (November to January) female lays 26–40 eggs and swallows them; they develop inside her stomach; 6–25 froglets are delivered through the mouth after a gestation period of 6–7 weeks

Related endangered species: Southern gastric-brooding frog (*Rheobatrachus vitellinus*) EN

Status: IUCN CR; not listed by CITES

Queensland

AUSTRALIA

Conondale Range   Blackall Range

New South Wales

See also: Disease **1:** 55; Frog, Green and Golden Bell **5:** 4; Frog, Tinkling **5:** 12

enabling it to swim powerfully, and it has upward-pointing eyes that help it see above the waterline.

The gastric-brooding frog's preferred habitat is rocky mountain creeks, where it spends most of the day hiding under rocks. It leaves the water to feed, going in search of live prey. Unlike many frogs, it does not have a protrusible tongue (one that can be pushed out), but catches its prey by lunging at it with an open mouth. During the breeding season males call females from the water's edge.

The slightly larger northern gastric-brooding frog lived in a similar habitat and also had a very restricted range, in the Clarke Mountains near Mackay in central coastal Queensland.

Mysterious Decline

The two gastric-brooding frogs are among several species that have declined in high-altitude habitats in Queensland. The declines are puzzling because they have occurred in protected areas where the forest has been conserved.

It is now thought that the declines are a result of a disease that has spread rapidly in Queensland as well as other parts of Australia and Central America. The disease is called

chytridiomycosis and is caused by a microscopic organism called a chytrid fungus.

The fungus is a parasite that invades the skin of amphibians, where it reproduces, digesting keratin, the fibrous protein in the outer layer of the skin. The tadpoles of frogs do not have keratin in their skin, except in the horny beak around their mouth, so they can carry the chytrid fungus without being adversely affected by it.

How the chytrid fungus kills frogs is not yet understood. One possibility is that it interferes with the passage of water and oxygen across a frog's skin; another is that it produces a substance that is toxic to frogs. It is not yet known how the disease found its way to Australia, although the most likely route was through amphibians introduced into the locality from elsewhere in the world.

The gastric-brooding frog

has prominent, upward-pointing eyes, enabling it to see above the waterline.

Glossary

Words in SMALL CAPITALS refer to other entries in the glossary.

Adaptation features of an animal that adjust it to its environment; may be produced by evolution—e.g., camouflage coloration

Adaptive radiation where a group of closely related animals (e.g., members of a FAMILY) have evolved differences from each other so that they can survive in different NICHES

Adhesive disks flattened disks on the tips of the fingers or toes of certain climbing AMPHIBIANS that enable them to cling to smooth, vertical surfaces

Adult a fully grown sexually mature animal; a bird in its final PLUMAGE

Algae primitive plants ranging from microscopic, single-celled forms to large forms, such as seaweeds, but lacking proper roots or leaves

Alpine living in mountainous areas, usually over 5,000 feet (1,500 m)

Ambient describing the conditions around an animal, e.g., the water temperature for a fish or the air temperature for a land animal

Amphibian any cold-blooded VERTEBRATE of the CLASS Amphibia, typically living on land but breathing in the water; e.g., frogs, toads, newts, salamanders

Amphibious able to live on both land and in water

Amphipod a type of CRUSTACEAN found on land and in both fresh and seawater

Anadromous fish that spend most of their life at sea but MIGRATE into fresh water for breeding, e.g., salmon

Annelid of the PHYLUM Annelida in which the body is made up of similar segments, e.g., earthworms, lugworms, leeches

Anterior the front part of an animal

Arachnid one of a group of ARTHROPODS of the CLASS Arachnida, characterized by simple eyes and four pairs of legs. Includes spiders and scorpions

Arboreal living in trees

Aristotle's lantern complex chewing apparatus of sea-urchins that includes five teeth

Arthropod the largest PHYLUM in the animal kingdom in terms of the number of SPECIES in it. Characterized by a hard, jointed EXOSKELETON and paired jointed legs. Includes INSECTS, spiders, crabs, etc.

Baleen horny substance commonly known as whalebone and growing as plates in the mouth of certain whales; used as a fringelike sieve for extracting plankton from seawater

Bill often called the beak: the jaws of a bird, consisting of two bony MANDIBLES, upper and lower, and their horny sheaths

Biodiversity the variety of SPECIES and the variation within them

Biome a major world landscape characterized by having similar plants and animals living in it, e.g., DESERT, jungle, forest

Biped any animal that walks on two legs. See QUADRUPED

Blowhole the nostril opening on the head of a whale through which it breathes

Breeding season the entire cycle of reproductive activity, from courtship, pair formation (and often establishment of territory) through nesting to independence of young

Bristle in birds a modified feather, with a bare or partly bare shaft, like a stiff hair; functions include protection, as with eyelashes of ostriches and hornbills, and touch sensors to help catch INSECTS, as with flycatchers

Brood the young hatching from a single CLUTCH of eggs

Browsing feeding on leaves of trees and shrubs

Cage bird A bird kept in captivity; in this set it usually refers to birds taken from the wild

Canine tooth a sharp stabbing tooth usually longer than the rest

Canopy continuous (closed) or broken (open) layer in forests produced by the intermingling of branches of trees

Carapace the upper part of a shell in a CHELONIAN

Carnivore meat-eating animal

Carrion rotting flesh of dead animals

Casque the raised portion on the head of certain REPTILES and birds

Catadromous fish that spend most of their life in fresh water but MIGRATE to the sea for SPAWNING, e.g., eels

Caudal fin the tail fin in fish

Cephalothorax a body region of CRUSTACEANS formed by the union of the head and THORAX. See PROSOMA

Chelicerae the first pair of appendages ("limbs") on the PROSOMA of spiders, scorpions, etc. Often equipped to inject venom

Chelonian any REPTILE of the ORDER Chelonia, including the tortoises and turtles, in which most of the body is enclosed in a bony capsule

Chrysalis the PUPA in moths and butterflies

Class a large TAXONOMIC group of related animals. MAMMALS, INSECTS, and REPTILES are all CLASSES of animals

Cloaca cavity in the pelvic region into which the alimentary canal, genital, and urinary ducts open

Cloud forest moist, high-altitude forest characterized by a dense UNDERSTORY and an abundance of ferns, mosses, and other plants growing on the trunks and branches of trees

Clutch a set of eggs laid by a female bird in a single breeding attempt

Cocoon the protective coat of many insect LARVAE before they develop into PUPAE or the silken covering secreted to protect the eggs

Colonial living together in a colony

Coniferous forest evergreen forests found in northern regions and mountainous areas, dominated by pines, spruce, and cedars

Costal riblike

Costal grooves grooves running around the body of some TERRESTRIAL salamanders; they conduct water from the ground to the upper parts of the body

Coverts small feathers covering the bases of a bird's main flight feathers on the wings and tail, providing a smooth, streamlined surface for flight

Crustacean member of a CLASS within the PHYLUM Arthropoda typified by five pairs of legs, two pairs of antennae, a joined head and THORAX, and calcerous deposits in the EXOSKELETON; e.g., crabs, shrimps, etc.

Deciduous forest dominated by trees that lose their leaves in winter (or in the dry season)

Deforestation the process of cutting down and removing trees for timber or to create open space for growing crops, grazing animals, etc.

Desert area of low rainfall typically with sparse scrub or grassland vegetation or lacking it altogether

Diatoms microscopic single-celled ALGAE

Dispersal the scattering of young animals going to live away from where they were born and brought up

Diurnal active during the day

DNA (deoxyribonucleic acid) the substance that makes up the main part of the chromosomes of all living things; contains the genetic code that is handed down from generation to generation

Domestication process of taming and breeding animals to provide help and useful products for humans

Dormancy a state in which—as a result of hormone action—growth is suspended and METABOLIC activity is reduced to a minimum

Dorsal relating to the back or spinal part of the body; usually the upper surface

Down soft, fluffy, insulating feathers with few or no shafts found after hatching on young birds and in ADULTS beneath the main feathers

Echolocation the process of perception based on reaction to the pattern of reflected sound waves (echos); occurs in bats

Ecology the study of plants and animals in relation to one another and to their surroundings

Ecosystem a whole system in which plants, animals, and their environment interact

Ectotherm animal that relies on external heat sources to raise body temperature; also known as "cold-blooded"

Edentate toothless; also any animals of the order Edentata, which includes anteaters, sloths, and armadillos

Endemic found only in one geographical area, nowhere else

Epitoke a form of marine ANNELID having particularly well developed swimming appendages

Estivation inactivity or greatly decreased activity during hot weather

Eutrophication an increase in the nutrient chemicals (nitrate, phosphate, etc.) in water, sometimes occurring naturally and sometimes caused by human activities, e.g., by the release of sewage or agricultural fertilizers

Exoskeleton a skeleton covering the outside of the body or situated in the skin, as found in some INVERTEBRATES

Explosive breeding in some AMPHIBIANS when breeding is completed over one or a very few days and nights

Extinction process of dying out at the end of which the very last individual dies, and the SPECIES is lost forever

Family a group of closely related SPECIES that often also look quite similar. Zoological FAMILY names always end in -idae. Also used to describe a social group within a SPECIES comprising parents and their offspring

Feral domestic animals that have gone wild and live independently of people

Flagship species A high-profile SPECIES, which (if present) is likely to be accompanied by many others that are typical of the habitat. (If a naval flagship is present, so is the rest of the fleet of warships and support vessels)

Fledging period the period between a young bird hatching and acquiring its first full set of feathers and being able to fly

Fledgling young bird that is capable of flight; in perching birds and some others it corresponds with the time of leaving the nest

Fluke either of the two lobes of the tail of a whale or related animal; also a type of flatworm, usually parasitic

Gamebird birds in the ORDER Galliformes (megapodes, cracids, grouse, partridges, quail, pheasants, and relatives); also used for any birds that may be legally hunted by humans

Gene the basic unit of heredity, enabling one generation to pass on characteristics to its offspring

Genus (**genera**, pl.) a group of closely related SPECIES

Gestation the period of pregnancy in MAMMALS, between fertilization of the egg and birth of the baby

Gill Respiratory organ that absorbs oxygen from the water. External gills occur in tadpoles. Internal gills occur in most fish

Harem a group of females living in the same territory and consorting with a single male

Hen any female bird

Herbivore an animal that eats plants (grazers and BROWSERS are herbivores)

Hermaphrodite an animal having both male and female reproductive organs

Herpetologist ZOOLOGIST who studies REPTILES and AMPHIBIANS

Hibernation becoming inactive in winter, with lowered body temperature to save energy. Hibernation takes place in a special nest or den called a hibernaculum

Homeotherm an animal that can maintain a high and constant body temperature by means of internal

processes; also called "warm-blooded"

Home range the area that an animal uses in the course of its normal activity

Hybrid offspring of two closely related SPECIES that can breed; it is sterile and so cannot produce offspring

Ichthyologist ZOOLOGIST specializing in the study of fish

Inbreeding breeding among closely related animals (e.g., cousins), leading to weakened genetic composition and reduced survival rates

Incubation the act of keeping the egg or eggs warm or the period from the laying of eggs to hatching

Indwellers ORGANISMS that live inside others, e.g., the California Bay pea crab, which lives in the tubes of some marine ANNELID worms, but do not act as PARASITES

Indigenous living naturally in a region; native (i.e., not an introduced SPECIES)

Insect any air-breathing ARTHROPOD of the CLASS Insecta, having a body divided into head, THORAX, and abdomen, three pairs of legs, and sometimes two pairs of wings

Insectivore animal that feeds on INSECTS. Also used as a group name for hedgehogs, shrews, moles, etc.

Interbreeding breeding between animals of different SPECIES, varieties, etc. within a single FAMILY or strain; Interbreeding can cause dilution of the GENE pool

Interspecific between SPECIES

Intraspecific between individuals of the same SPECIES

Invertebrates animals that have no backbone (or other bones) inside their body, e.g., mollusks, INSECTS, jellyfish, crabs

Iridescent displaying glossy colors produced (e.g., in bird PLUMAGE) not as a result of pigments but by the splitting of sunlight into light of different wavelengths; rainbows are made in the same way

Joey a young kangaroo living in its mother's pouch

Juvenile a young animal that has not yet reached breeding age

Keel a ridge along the CARAPACE of certain turtles or a ridge on the scales of some REPTILES

Keratin tough, fibrous material that forms hair, feathers, nails, and

protective plates on the skin of VERTEBRATE animals

Keystone species a SPECIES on which many other SPECIES are wholly or partially dependent

Krill PLANKTONIC shrimps

Labyrinth specialized auxiliary (extra) breathing organ found in some fish

Larva an immature form of an animal that develops into an ADULT form through METAMORPHOSIS

Lateral line system a system of pores running along a fish's body. These pores lead to nerve endings that allow a fish to sense vibrations in the water and help it locate prey, detect PREDATORS, avoid obstacles, and so on. Also found in AMPHIBIANS

Lek communal display area where male birds of some SPECIES gather to attract and mate with females

Livebearer animal that gives birth to fully developed young (usually refers to REPTILES or fish)

Mammal any animal of the CLASS Mammalia—warm-blooded VERTEBRATE having mammary glands in the female that produce milk with which it nurses its young. The class includes bats, primates, rodents, and whales

Mandible upper or lower part of a bird's beak or BILL; also the jawbone in VERTEBRATES; in INSECTS and other ARTHROPODS mandibles are mouth parts mostly used for biting and chewing

Mantle cavity a space in the body of mollusks that contains the breathing organs

Marine living in the sea

Matriarch senior female member of a social group

Metabolic rate the rate at which chemical activities occur within animals, including the exchange of gasses in respiration and the liberation of energy from food

Metamorphosis the transformation of a LARVA into an ADULT

Migration movement from one place to another and back again; usually seasonal

Molt the process in which a bird sheds its feathers and replaces them with new ones; some MAMMALS, REPTILES, and ARTHROPODS regularly molt, shedding hair, skin, or outer layers

Monotreme egg-laying MAMMAL, e.g., platypus

Montane in a mountain environment

Natural selection the process

whereby individuals with the most appropriate ADAPTATIONS are more successful than other individuals and therefore survive to produce more offspring. Natural selection is the main process driving evolution in which animals and plants are challenged by natural effects (such as predation and bad weather), resulting in survival of the fittest

Nematocyst the stinging part of animals such as jellyfish, usually found on the tentacles

Nestling a young bird still in the nest and dependent on its parents

New World the Americas

Niche part of a habitat occupied by an ORGANISM, defined in terms of all aspects of its lifestyle

Nocturnal active at night

Nomadic animals that have no fixed home, but wander continuously

Noseleaf fleshy structures around the face of bats; helps focus ULTRASOUNDS used for ECHOLOCATION

Ocelli markings on an animal's body that resemble eyes. Also, the tiny, simple eyes of some INSECTS, spiders, CRUSTACEANS, mollusks, etc.

Old World non-American continents

Olfaction sense of smell

Operculum a cover consisting of bony plates that covers the GILLS of fish

Omnivore an animal that eats a wide range of both animal and vegetable food

Order a subdivision of a CLASS of animals, consisting of a series of animal FAMILIES

Organism any member of the animal or plant kingdom; a body that has life

Ornithologist ZOOLOGIST specializing in the study of birds

Osteoderms bony plates beneath the scales of some REPTILES, particularly crocodilians

Oviparous producing eggs that hatch outside the body of the mother (in fish, REPTILES, birds, and MONOTREMES)

Parasite an animal or plant that lives on or within the body of another (the host) from which it obtains nourishment. The host is often harmed by the association

Passerine any bird of the ORDER Passeriformes; includes SONGBIRDS

Pedipalps small, paired leglike appendages immediately in front of the first pair of walking legs of spiders and other ARACHNIDS. Used by males for transferring sperm to the females

Pelagic living in the upper waters of the open sea or large lakes

Pheromone scent produced by animals to enable others to find and recognize them

Photosynthesis the production of food in green plants using sunlight as an energy source and water plus carbon dioxide as raw materials

Phylum zoological term for a major grouping of animal CLASSES. The whole animal kingdom is divided into about 30 PHYLA, of which the VERTEBRATES form part of just one

Placenta the structure that links an embryo to its mother during pregnancy, allowing exchange of chemicals between them

Plankton animals and plants drifting in open water; many are minute

Plastron the lower shell of CHELONIANS

Plumage the covering of feathers on a bird's body

Plume a long feather used for display, as in a bird of paradise

Polygamous where an individual has more than one mate in one BREEDING SEASON. Monogamous animals have only a single mate

Polygynous where a male mates with several females in one BREEDING SEASON

Polyp individual ORGANISM that lives as part of a COLONY—e.g., a coral—with a saclike body opening only by the mouth that is usually surrounded by a ring of tentacles

Population a distinct group of animals of the same SPECIES or all the animals of that SPECIES

Posterior the hind end or behind another structure

Predator an animal that kills live prey

Prehensile capable of grasping

Primary forest forest that has always been forest and has not been cut down and regrown at some time

Primates a group of MAMMALS that includes monkeys, apes, and ourselves

Prosoma the joined head and THORAX of a spider, scorpion, or horseshoe crab

Pupa an INSECT in the stage of METAMORPHOSIS between a caterpillar (LARVA) and an ADULT (imago)

Quadruped any animal that walks on four legs

Range the total geographical area over which a SPECIES is distributed

Raptor bird with hooked beak and strong feet with sharp claws (talons) for seizing, killing, and dealing with prey; also known as birds of prey. The term usually refers to daytime birds of prey (eagles, hawks, falcons, and relatives) but sometimes also includes NOCTURNAL owls

Regurgitate (of a bird) to vomit partly digested food either to feed NESTLINGS or to rid itself of bones, fur, or other indigestible parts, or (in some seabirds) to scare off PREDATORS

Reptile any member of the cold-blooded CLASS Reptilia, such as crocodiles, lizards, snakes, tortoises, turtles, and tuataras; characterized by an external covering of scales or horny plates. Most are egg-layers, but some give birth to fully developed young

Roost place that a bird or bat regularly uses for sleeping

Ruminant animals that eat vegetation and later bring it back from the stomach to chew again ("chewing the cud") to assist its digestion by microbes in the stomach

Savanna open grasslands with scattered trees and low rainfall, usually in warm areas

Scapulars the feathers of a bird above its shoulders

Scent chemicals produced by animals to leave smell messages for others to find and interpret

Scrub vegetation dominated by shrubs—woody plants usually with more than one stem

Scute horny plate covering live body tissue underneath

Secondary forest trees that have been planted or grown up on cleared ground

Sedge grasslike plant

Shorebird Plovers, sandpipers, and relatives (known as waders in Britain, Australia, and some other areas)

Slash-and-burn agriculture method of farming in which the unwanted vegetation is cleared by cutting down and burning

Social behavior interactions between individuals within the same SPECIES, e.g., courtship

Songbird member of major bird group of PASSERINES

Spawning the laying and fertilizing of eggs by fish and AMPHIBIANS and some mollusks

Speciation the origin of SPECIES; the diverging of two similar ORGANISMS

through reproduction down through the generations into different forms resulting in a new SPECIES

Species a group of animals that look similar and can breed with each other to produce fertile offspring

Steppe open grassland in parts of the world where the climate is too harsh for trees to grow

Subspecies a subpopulation of a single SPECIES whose members are similar to each other but differ from the typical form for that SPECIES; often called a race

Substrate a medium to which fixed animals are attached under water, such as rocks onto which barnacles and mussels are attached, or plants are anchored in, e.g., gravel, mud, or sand in which AQUATIC plants have their roots embedded

Substratum see SUBSTRATE

Swim bladder a gas or air-filled bladder in fish; by taking in or exhaling air, the fish can alter its buoyancy

Symbiosis a close relationship between members of two SPECIES from which both partners benefit

Taxonomy the branch of biology concerned with classifying ORGANISMS into groups according to similarities in their structure, origins, or behavior. The categories, in order of increasing broadness, are: SPECIES, GENUS, FAMILY, ORDER, CLASS, PHYLUM

Terrestrial living on land

Territory defended space

Test an external covering or "shell" of an INVERTEBRATE such as a sea-urchin; it is in fact an internal skeleton just below the skin

Thorax (**thoracic**, adj.) in an INSECT the middle region of the body between the head and the abdomen. It bears the wings and three pairs of walking legs

Torpor deep sleep accompanied by lowered body temperature and reduced METABOLIC RATE

Translocation transferring members of a SPECIES from one location to another

Tundra open grassy or shrub-covered lands of the far north

Underfur fine hairs forming a dense, woolly mass close to the skin and underneath the outer coat of stiff hairs in MAMMALS

Understory the layer of shrubs,

herbs, and small trees found beneath the forest CANOPY

Ungulate one of a large group of hoofed animals such as pigs, deer, cattle, and horses; mostly HERBIVORES

Uterus womb in which embryos of MAMMALS develop

Ultrasounds sounds that are too high-pitched for humans to hear

UV-B radiation component of ultraviolet radiation from the sun that is harmful to living ORGANISMS because it breaks up DNA

Vane the bladelike main part of a typical bird feather extending from either side of its shaft (midrib)

Ventral of or relating to the front part or belly of an animal (see DORSAL)

Vertebrate animal with a backbone (e.g., fish, MAMMAL, REPTILE), usually with skeleton made of bones, but sometimes softer cartilage

Vestigial a characteristic with little or no use, but derived from one that was well developed in an ancestral form; e.g., the "parson's nose" (the fatty end portion of the tail when a fowl is cooked) is the compressed bones from the long tail of the reptilian ancestor of birds

Viviparous (of most MAMMALS and a few other VERTEBRATES) giving birth to active young rather than laying eggs

Waterfowl members of the bird FAMILY Anatidae, the swans, geese, and ducks; sometimes used to include other groups of wild AQUATIC birds

Wattle fleshy protuberance, usually near the base of a bird's BILL

Wingbar line of contrasting feathers on a bird's wing

Wing case one of the protective structures formed from the first pair of nonfunctional wings, which are used to protect the second pair of functional wings in INSECTS such as beetles

Wintering ground the area where a migrant spends time outside the BREEDING SEASON

Yolk part of the egg that contains nourishment for a growing embryo

Zooid individual animal in a colony; usually applied to corals or bryozoa (sea-mats)

Zoologist person who studies animals

Zoology the study of animals

Further Reading

Mammals
Macdonald, David, *The Encyclopedia of Mammals*, Barnes & Noble, New York, U.S., 2001

Payne, Roger, *Among Whales*, Bantam Press, U.S., 1996

Reeves, R. R., and Leatherwood, S., *The Sierra Club Handbook of Whales and Dolphins of the World*, Sierra Club, U.S., 1983

Sherrow, Victoria, and Cohen, Sandee, *Endangered Mammals of North America*, Twenty-First Century Books, U.S., 1995

Whitaker, J. O., *Audubon Society Field Guide to North American Mammals*, Alfred A. Knopf, New York, U.S., 1996

Birds
Attenborough, David, *The Life of Birds*, BBC Books, London, U.K., 1998

BirdLife International, *Threatened Birds of the World*, Lynx Edicions, Barcelona, Spain and BirdLife International, Cambridge, U.K., 2000

del Hoyo, J., Elliott, A., and Sargatal, J., eds. *Handbook of Birds of the World* Vols 1 to 6, Lynx Edicions, Barcelona, Spain, 1992–2001

Sayre, April Pulley, *Endangered Birds of North America*, Scientific American Sourcebooks, Twenty-First Century Books, U.S., 1977

Scott, Shirley L., ed., *A Field Guide to the Birds of North America*, National Geographic, U.S., 1999

Stattersfield, A., Crosby, M., Long, A., and Wege, D., eds., *Endemic Bird Areas of the World: Priorities for Biodiversity Conservation*, BirdLife International, Cambridge, U.K., 1998

Thomas, Peggy, *Bird Alert: Science of Saving*, Twenty-First Century Books, U.S., 2000

Fish
Bannister, Keith, and Campbell, Andrew, *The Encyclopedia of Aquatic Life*, Facts On File, New York, U.S., 1997

Buttfield, Helen, *The Secret Lives of Fishes*, Abrams, U.S., 2000

Reptiles and Amphibians
Corbett, Keith, *Conservation of European Reptiles and Amphibians*, Christopher Helm, London, U.K., 1989

Corton, Misty, *Leopard and Other South African Tortoises*, Carapace Press, London, U.K., 2000

Hofrichter, Robert, *Amphibians: The World of Frogs, Toads, Salamanders, and Newts*, Firefly Books, Canada, 2000

Stafford, Peter, *Snakes*, Natural History Museum, London, U.K., 2000

Insects
Borror, Donald J., and White, Richard E., *A Field Guide to Insects: America, North of Mexico*, Houghton Mifflin, New York, U.S., 1970

Pyle, Robert Michael, *National Audubon Society Field Guide to North American Butterflies*, Alfred A. Knopf, New York, U.S., 1995

General
Adams, Douglas, and Carwardine, Mark, *Last Chance to See*, Random House, London, U.K., 1992

Allaby, Michael, *The Concise Oxford Dictionary of Ecology*, Oxford University Press, Oxford, U.K., 1998

Douglas, Dougal, and others, *Atlas of Life on Earth*, Barnes & Noble, New York, U.S., 2001

National Wildlife Federation, *Endangered Species: Wild and Rare*, McGraw-Hill, U.S., 1996

Websites

http://www.abcbirds.org/ American Bird Conservancy. Articles, information about campaigns and bird conservation in the Americas

http://elib.cs.berkeley.edu/aw/ AmphibiaWeb information about amphibians and their conservation

http://animaldiversity.ummz.umich.edu/ University of Michigan Museum of Zoology animal diversity web. Search for pictures and information about animals by class, family, and common name. Includes glossary

www.beachside.org sea turtle preservation society

http://www.birdlife.net BirdLife International, an alliance of conservation organizations working in more than 100 countries to save birds and their habitats

http://www.surfbirds.com Articles, mystery photographs, news, book reviews, birding polls, and more

http://www.birds.cornell.edu/ Cornell University. Courses, news, nest-box cam

http://www.cites.org/ CITES and IUCN listings. Search for animals by scientific name of order, family, genus, species, or common name. Location by country and explanation of reasons for listings

www.ufl.edu/natsci/herpetology/crocs.htm crocodile site, including a chat room

www.darwinfoundation.org/ Charles Darwin Research Center

http://www.open.cc.uk/daptf DAPTF–Declining Amphibian Population Task Force. Providing information and data about amphibian declines. (International Director, Professor Tim Halliday, is co-author of this set)

http://www.ucmp.berkeley.edu/echinodermata the echinoderm phylum—starfish, sea-urchins, etc.

http://endangered.fws.gov information about endangered animals and plants from the U.S. Fish and Wildlife Service, the organization in charge of 94 million acres of wildlife refuges

http://forests.org/ includes forest conservation answers to queries

www.traffic.org/turtles freshwater turtles

www.iucn.org details of species, IUCN listings and IUCN publications

http://www.pbs.org/journeytoamazonia the Amazonian rain forest and its unrivaled biodiversity

http://www.audubon.org National Audubon Society, named after the ornithologist and wildlife artist John James Audubon (1785–1851). Sections on education, local Audubon societies, and bird identification

www.nccnsw.org.au site for threatened Australian species

http://cmc-ocean.org facts, figures, and quizzes about marine life

http://wwwl.nature.nps.gov/wv/ The U.S. National Park Service wildlife and plants site. Factsheets on all kinds of animals found in the parks

www.ewt.org.za endangered South African wildlife

http://www.panda.org World Wide Fund for Nature (WWF). Newsroom, press releases, government reports, campaigns. Themed photogallery

http://www.greenchannel.com/wwt/ Wildfowl and Wetlands Trust (U.K.). Founded by artist and naturalist Sir Peter Scott, the trust aims to preserve wetlands for rare waterbirds. Includes information on places to visit and threatened waterbird species

http://wdcs.org/ Whale and Dolphin Conservation Society site. News, projects, and campaigns. Sightings database

99

List of Animals by Group

Listed below are the common names of the animals featured in the A–Z part of this set grouped by their class, i.e., Mammals, Birds, Fish, Reptiles, Amphibians, and Insects and Invertebrates.

Bold numbers indicate the volume number and are followed by the first page number of the two-page illustrated main entry in the set.

Mammals
addax **2:**4
anoa, mountain **2:**20
anteater, giant **2:**24
antelope, Tibetan **2:**26
armadillo, giant **2:**30
ass
   African wild **2:**34
   Asiatic wild **2:**36
aye-aye **2:**42
babirusa **2:**44
baboon, gelada **2:**46
bandicoot, western barred **2:**48
banteng **2:**50
bat
   ghost **2:**56
   gray **2:**58
   greater horseshoe **2:**60
   greater mouse-eared **2:**62
   Kitti's hog-nosed **2:**64
   Morris's **2:**66
bear
   grizzly **2:**68
   polar **2:**70
   sloth **2:**72
   spectacled **2:**74
beaver, Eurasian **2:**76
bison
   American **2:**86
   European **2:**88
blackbuck **2:**94
camel, wild bactrian **3:**24
cat, Iriomote **3:**30
cheetah **3:**40
chimpanzee **3:**42
   pygmy **3:**44
chinchilla, short-tailed **3:**46
cow, Steller's sea **3:**70
cuscus, black-spotted **3:**86
deer
   Chinese water **4:**6
   Kuhl's **4:**8
   Père David's **4:**10
   Siberian musk **4:**12
desman, Russian **4:**14
dhole **4:**16
dog
   African wild **4:**22

bush **4:**24
dolphin
   Amazon river **4:**26
   Yangtze river **4:**28
dormouse
   common **4:**30
   garden **4:**32
   Japanese **4:**34
drill **4:**40
dugong **4:**46
duiker, Jentink's **4:**48
dunnart, Kangaroo Island **4:**50
echidna, long-beaked **4:**60
elephant
   African **4:**64
   Asian **4:**66
elephant-shrew, golden-rumped **4:**68
ferret, black-footed **4:**72
flying fox
   Rodrigues (Rodriguez) **4:**84
   Ryukyu **4:**86
fossa **4:**90
fox, swift **4:**92
gaur **5:**18
gazelle, dama **5:**20
gibbon, black **5:**26
giraffe, reticulated **5:**30
glider, mahogany **5:**32
gorilla
   mountain **5:**38
   western lowland **5:**40
gymnure, Hainan **5:**48
hare, hispid **5:**50
hippopotamus, pygmy **5:**52
horse, Przewalski's wild **5:**58
hutia, Jamaican **5:**64
hyena
   brown **5:**66
   spotted **5:**68
ibex, Nubian **5:**70
indri **5:**84
jaguar **5:**86
koala **6:**10
kouprey **6:**14
kudu, greater **6:**16
lemur
   hairy-eared dwarf **6:**22
   Philippine flying **6:**24
   ruffed **6:**26
leopard **6:**28
   clouded **6:**30
   snow **6:**32
lion, Asiatic **6:**34
loris, slender **6:**46
lynx, Iberian **6:**52
macaque
   barbary **6:**54
   Japanese **6:**56
manatee, Florida **6:**68
markhor **6:**72
marten, pine **6:**74
mink, European **6:**78

mole, marsupial **6:**80
mole-rat
   Balkans **6:**82
   giant **6:**84
monkey
   douc **6:**86
   Goeldi's **6:**88
   proboscis **6:**90
mouse, St. Kilda **6:**92
mulgara **6:**94
numbat **7:**14
nyala, mountain **7:**18
ocelot, Texas **7:**20
okapi **7:**22
orang-utan **7:**26
oryx
   Arabian **7:**28
   scimitar-horned **7:**30
otter
   European **7:**32
   giant **7:**34
   sea **7:**36
ox, Vu Quang **7:**44
panda
   giant **7:**48
   lesser **7:**50
pangolin, long-tailed **7:**52
panther, Florida **7:**54
pig, Visayan warty **7:**68
pika, steppe **7:**74
platypus **7:**82
porpoise, harbor **7:**86
possum, Leadbeater's **7:**88
potoroo, long-footed **7:**90
prairie dog, black-tailed **7:**92
pygmy-possum, mountain **8:**4
quagga **8:**8
rabbit
   Amami **8:**12
   volcano **8:**14
rat, black **8:**24
rhinoceros
   black **8:**26
   great Indian **8:**28
   Javan **8:**30
   Sumatran **8:**32
   white **8:**34
rock-wallaby, Prosperine **8:**36
saiga **8:**42
sea lion, Steller's **8:**62
seal
   Baikal **8:**70
   gray **8:**72
   Hawaiian monk **8:**74
   Mediterranean monk **8:**76
   northern fur **8:**78
sheep, barbary **8:**88
shrew, giant otter **8:**90
sifaka, golden-crowned **8:**92
sloth, maned **9:**6
solenodon, Cuban **9:**16
souslik, European **9:**18
squirrel, Eurasian red **9:**28

tahr, Nilgiri **9:**46
takin **9:**50
tamarin, golden lion **9:**52
tapir
   Central American **9:**56
   Malayan **9:**58
tenrec, aquatic **9:**64
thylacine **9:**66
tiger **9:**68
tree-kangaroo, Goodfellow's **10:**4
vicuña **10:**28
whale
   blue **10:**40
   fin **10:**42
   gray **10:**44
   humpback **10:**46
   killer **10:**48
   minke **10:**50
   northern right **10:**52
   sei **10:**54
   sperm **10:**56
   white **10:**58
wildcat **10:**62
wolf
   Ethiopian **10:**64
   Falkland Island **10:**66
   gray **10:**68
   maned **10:**70
   red **10:**72
wolverine **10:**74
wombat, northern hairy-nosed **10:**76
yak, wild **10:**90
zebra
   Grevy's **10:**92
   mountain **10:**94

Birds
akiapolaau **2:**6
albatross, wandering **2:**8
amazon, St. Vincent **2:**14
asity, yellow-bellied **2:**32
auk, great **2:**38
barbet, toucan **2:**54
bellbird, three-wattled **2:**82
bird of paradise, blue **2:**84
bittern, Eurasian **2:**90
blackbird, saffron-cowled **2:**92
bowerbird, Archbold's **3:**8
bustard, great **3:**10
cassowary, southern **3:**28
cockatoo, salmon-crested **3:**52
condor, California **3:**60
coot, horned **3:**62
cormorant, Galápagos **3:**64
corncrake **3:**66
courser, Jerdon's **3:**68
crane, whooping **3:**76
crow, Hawaiian **3:**82
curlew, Eskimo **3:**84
dipper, rufous-throated **4:**18

dodo **4:**20
duck
  Labrador **4:**42
  white-headed **4:**44
eagle
  harpy **4:**52
  Philippine **4:**54
  Spanish imperial **4:**56
finch
  Gouldian **4:**74
  mangrove **4:**76
firecrown, Juan Fernández **4:**78
flamingo, Andean **4:**80
flycatcher, Pacific royal **4:**82
fody, Mauritius **4:**88
grebe, Atitlán **5:**42
guan, horned **5:**44
gull, lava **5:**46
honeyeater, regent **5:**54
hornbill, writhed **5:**56
huia **5:**60
hummingbird, bee **5:**62
ibis, northern bald **5:**72
kagu **5:**88
kakapo **5:**90
kea **5:**92
kestrel
  lesser **5:**94
  Mauritius **6:**4
kite, red **6:**6
kiwi, brown **6:**8
lark, Raso **6:**18
lovebird, black-cheeked **6:**48
macaw
  hyacinth **6:**58
  Spix's **6:**60
magpie-robin, Seychelles
  6:62
malleefowl **6:**64
manakin, black-capped
  6:66
mesite, white-breasted
  6:76
murrelet, Japanese **7:**4
nene **7:**10
nuthatch, Algerian **7:**16
owl
  Blakiston's eagle **7:**38
  Madagascar red **7:**40
  spotted **7:**42
parrot, night **7:**58
peafowl, Congo **7:**60
pelican, Dalmatian **7:**62
penguin, Galápagos **7:**64
petrel, Bermuda **7:**66
pigeon
  pink **7:**70
  Victoria crowned **7:**72
pitta, Gurney's **7:**78
plover, piping **7:**84
quetzal, resplendent **8:**10
rail, Guam **8:**18
rockfowl, white-necked **8:**38
sandpiper, spoon-billed **8:**54

scrub-bird, noisy **8:**56
sea-eagle, Steller's **8:**64
siskin, red **8:**94
spatuletail, marvelous **9:**20
spoonbill, black-faced **9:**26
starling, Bali **9:**30
stilt, black **9:**32
stork, greater adjutant **9:**34
swallow, blue **9:**42
swan, trumpeter **9:**44
takahe **9:**48
tanager, seven-colored **9:**54
teal, Baikal **9:**62
tragopan, Temminck's **9:**94
turaco, Bannerman's **10:**10
vanga, helmet **10:**26
vireo, black-capped **10:**32
vulture, Cape griffon **10:**34
warbler
  aquatic **10:**36
  Kirtland's **10:**38
woodpecker
  ivory-billed **10:**78
  red-cockaded **10:**80
wren, Zapata **10:**86

Fish
anchovy, freshwater **2:**16
angelfish, masked **2:**18
archerfish, western **2:**28
barb, bandula **2:**52
caracolera, mojarra **3:**26
catfish, giant **3:**32
cavefish, Alabama **3:**34
characin, blind cave **3:**38
cichlids, Lake Victoria
  haplochromine **3:**48
cod
  Atlantic **3:**54
  trout **3:**56
coelacanth **3:**58
dace, mountain blackside
  3:90
danio, barred **3:**94
darter, watercress **4:**4
dragon fish **4:**36
eel, lesser spiny **4:**62
galaxias, swan **5:**16
goby, dwarf pygmy **5:**34
goodeid, gold sawfin **5:**36
ikan temoleh **5:**82
lungfish, Australian **6:**50
paddlefish **7:**46
paradisefish, ornate **7:**56
pirarucu **7:**76
platy, Cuatro Ciénegas **7:**80
pupfish, Devil's Hole **7:**94
rainbowfish, Lake Wanam **8:**20
rasbora, vateria flower **8:**22
rocky, eastern province **8:**40
salmon, Danube **8:**52
seahorse, Knysna **8:**68
shark
  basking **8:**80

great white **8:**82
silver **8:**84
whale **8:**86
sturgeon, common **9:**36
sucker, razorback **9:**38
sunfish, spring pygmy **9:**40
toothcarp, Valencia **9:**80
totoaba **9:**92
tuna, northern bluefin **10:**8
xenopoecilus **10:**88

Reptiles
alligator
  American **2:**10
  Chinese **2:**12
boa
  Jamaican **3:**4
  Madagascar **3:**6
chameleon, south central lesser
  3:36
crocodile, American **3:**80
dragon, southeastern lined
  earless **4:**38
gecko, Round Island day **5:**22
gharial **5:**24
Gila monster **5:**28
iguana
  Fijian crested **5:**74
  Galápagos land **5:**76
  Galápagos marine **5:**78
  Grand Cayman blue rock **5:**80
Komodo dragon **6:**12
lizard
  blunt-nosed leopard **6:**36
  flat-tailed horned **6:**38
  Ibiza wall **6:**40
  sand **6:**42
python, woma **8:**6
racer, Antiguan **8:**16
skink, pygmy blue-tongued
  9:4
snake
  eastern indigo **9:**10
  leopard **9:**12
  San Francisco garter **9:**14
tortoise **9:**82
  Egyptian **9:**84
  Desert **9:**82
  Galápagos giant **9:**86
  geometric **9:**88
  plowshare **9:**90
tuatara **10:**6
turtle
  Alabama red-bellied **10:**12
  bog **10:**14
  Chinese three-striped box
    10:16
  hawksbill **10:**18
  pig-nosed **10:**20
  western swamp **10:**22
  yellow-blotched sawback
    map **10:**24
viper, Milos **10:**30
whiptail, St. Lucia **10:**60

Amphibians
axolotl **2:**40
frog
  gastric-brooding **4:**94
  green and golden bell **5:**4
  Hamilton's **5:**6
  harlequin **5:**8
  red-legged **5:**10
  tinkling **5:**12
  tomato **5:**14
mantella, golden **6:**70
newt, great crested **7:**12
olm **7:**24
salamander
  California tiger **8:**44
  Japanese giant **8:**46
  Ouachita red-backed **8:**48
  Santa Cruz long-toed **8:**50
toad
  golden **9:**70
  Mallorcan midwife **9:**72
  natterjack **9:**74
  western **9:**76
toadlet, corroboree **9:**78

Insects and Invertebrates
ant, European red wood **2:**22
beetle
  blue ground **2:**78
  hermit **2:**80
butterfly
  Apollo **3:**12
  Avalon hairstreak **3:**14
  birdwing **3:**16
  Hermes copper **3:**18
  large blue **3:**20
  large copper **3:**22
clam, giant **3:**50
crab
  California Bay pea **3:**72
  horseshoe **3:**74
crayfish, noble **3:**78
cushion star **3:**88
damselfly, southern **3:**92
earthworm, giant gippsland
  4:58
emerald, orange-spotted **4:**70
leech, medicinal **6:**20
longicorn, cerambyx **6:**44
mussel, freshwater **7:**6
nemertine, Rodrigues **7:**8
sea anemone, starlet **8:**58
sea fan, broad **8:**60
sea-urchin, edible **8:**66
snail, *Partula* **9:**8
spider
  great raft **9:**22
  Kauai cave wolf **9:**24
tarantula, red-kneed **9:**60
worm
  palolo **10:**82
  velvet **10:**84

Set Index

A **bold** number indicates the volume number and is followed by the relevant page number or numbers (e.g., **1:**52, 74).

Animals that are main entries in the A–Z part of the set are listed under their common names, alternative common names, and scientific names. Animals that appear in the data panels as Related endangered species are also listed under their common and scientific names.

Common names in **bold** (e.g., **addax**) indicate that the animal is a main entry in the set. Underlined page numbers (e.g., **2:**12) indicate the first page of the two-page main entry on that animal.

Italic volume and page references (e.g., *1:57*) indicate illustrations of animals in other parts of the set.

References to animals that are listed by the IUCN as Extinct (EX), Extinct in the Wild (EW), or Critically Endangered (CR) are found under those headings.

spp. means species.

A

Aceros spp. **5:**56
 A. leucocephalus **5:**5
Acestrura bombus **4:**78
Acinonyx jubatus **3:**40
Acipenser
 A. nudiventris **9:**36
 A. sturio **9:**36
Acrantophis madagascariensis **3:**6
Acrocephalus spp. **10:**36
 A. paludicola **10:**36
adaptation, reproductive strategies **1:**25
addax 2:4
Addax nasomaculatus **2:**4
Adelocosa anops **9:**24
Adranichthyis kruyti **10:**88
Aegialia concinna **2:**80
Aegypius monachus **10:**34
Aepypodius bruijnii **6:**64
Afropavo congensis **7:**60
Agapornis
 A. fischeri **6:**48
 A. nigrigenis **6:**48
Agelaius xanthomus **2:**92
Aglaeactis aliciae **4:**78
agricultural land use **1:**38, 61
agricultural practices **1:**52, 74; **2:**60, 63, 73, 92; **3:**10, 13, 67, 85; **4:**19, 24, 75; **5:**50, 94; **6:**6, 36, 38, 48, 82, 95; **7:**12, 19; **8:**95; **9:**4, 18; **10:**14, 34
Ailuroedus dentirostris **3:**8
Ailuropoda melanoleuca **7:**48
Ailurus fulgens **7:**50
akiapolaau 2:6
ala Balik **8:**52
Alabama **3:**34
alala **3:**82
Alauda razae **6:**18

albatross
 various **2:**9
 wandering 2:8
Algeria **7:**16
alien species **1:**71; **2:**7, 56, 77; **3:**27, 65, 83; **4:**15, 20, 50, 76, 78, 79, 88; **5:**6, 11, 17, 22, 36, 43, 46, 50, 61, 64, 74, 76, 88, 92; **6:**8, 19, 62, 65, 78, 80, 94; **7:**5, 9, 10, 14, 59, 66, 70, 82, 90; **8:**12, 19, 20, 40, 16; **9:**9, 16, 28, 32, 38, 48, 72, 81, 88; **10:**60, 87, 88
Alligator
 A. mississippiensis **2:**10
 A. sinensis **2:**12
alligator
 American 2:10
 Chinese 2:12
Allocebus trichotis **6:**22
Allotoca maculata **5:**36
Alsophis spp. **8:**16
 A. antiguae **8:**16
Alytes muletensis **9:**72
Amandava formosa **4:**74
amarillo **5:**36
amazon
 St. Vincent 2:14
 various **2:**14
Amazona spp. **2:**14
 A. guildingii **2:**14
Amblyopsis
 A. rosae **3:**34
 A. spelaea **3:**34
Amblyornis flavifrons **3:**8
Amblyrhynchus cristatus **5:**78
Ambystoma
 A. macrodactylum croceum **8:**51
 A. mexicanum **2:**40
Amdystoma spp. **8:**44
 A. californiense **8:**44
Ameca splendens **5:**36

Ammotragus lervia **8:**88
amphibians **1:**76
 diversity **1:**76
 risks **1:**78
 strategies **1:**76
 see also List of Animals by Group, page 100
Anas spp. **9:**62
 A. formosa **9:**62
 A. laysanensis **7:**10
 A. wyvilliana **7:**10
anchovy, freshwater 2:16
Andes **2:**74; **3:**46; **4:**80; **10:**28
Andrias
 A. davidianus **8:**46
 A. japonicus **8:**46
anemone *see* sea anemone
angelfish
 masked 2:18
 resplendent pygmy **2:**19
Ångola **10:**94
angonoka **9:**90
animal products **1:**46; **3:**28, 75; **10:**42, 58
anoa
 lowland **2:**20; **6:**14
 mountain 2:20
Anoa mindorensis **2:**20
Anodorhynchus spp. **6:**60
 A. hyacinthus **6:**58
Anser erythropus **7:**10
ant, European red wood 2:22
anteater
 banded **7:**14
 fairy **2:**25
 giant 2:24
 marsupial **7:**14
 scaly **7:**52
Anthornis melanocephala **5:**54
Anthracoceros
 A. marchei **5:**56
 A. montani **5:**56
Antigua **8:**16
Antilope cervicapra **2:**94
Antilophia bokermanni **6:**66
aoudad **8:**88
ape, barbary **6:**54
Aplonis spp. **9:**30
Apodemus sylvaticus hirtensis **6:**92
Apteryx spp. **6:**9
 A. mantelli **6:**8
aquaculture **8:**55
aquarium trade **1:**49; **4:**36; **8:**23, 69, 84
Aquila spp. **4:**56
 A. adalberti **4:**56
Aramidopsis palteni **3:**66
arapaima **7:**76
Arapaima gigas **7:**76
archerfish
 few-scaled **2:**28
 large-scaled **2:**28

 western **2:**28
Archiboldia papuensis **3:**8
archipelagos **1:**32
 see also islands
Arctic **2:**70
Arctic Ocean **10:**58
Arctocephalus spp. **8:**62, 78
Ardeotis nigriceps **3:**10
Argentina **3:**46; 62; **4:**18
Arizona **3:**60
armadillo
 giant 2:30
 various **2:**30
arowana, Asian **4:**36
artificial fertilization **1:**88
Asia **3:**10, 66; **6:**20
asity
 Schlegel's **2:**32
 yellow-bellied 2:32
Aspidites ramsayi **8:**6
ass
 African wild 2:34; **8:**8
 Asiatic wild 2:36; **8:**8
 half- **2:**36
 Syrian wild *1:37*
Astacus astacus **3:**78
Asterina phylactica **3:**88
Astyanax mexicanus **3:**38
Atelopus varius **5:**8
Atlantic Ocean **3:**54, 88; **8:**72, 76, 80; **9:**36; **10:**8, 40, 43
Atlantisia rogersi **3:**66
Atlapetes flaviceps **4:**76
Atrichornis
 A. clamosus **8:**56
 A. rufescens **8:**56
auk, great 2:38
aurochs *1:37*
Australia **2:**16, 28, 48, 56; **3:**16, 28, 38, 46, 50, 58, 74, 94; **5:**12, 32, 54; **6:**10, 51, 64, 80, 94; **7:**14, 58, 82, 88, 90; **8:**4, 6, 36, 56; **9:**4, 66, 78; **10:**20, 22, 77
Austroglanis barnardi **3:**32
avadavat, green **4:**74
avahi **5:**84; **8:**93
Avahi occidentalis **5:**84; **8:**93
Axis kuhlii **4:**8
axolotl 2:40; **8:**44
aye-aye 2:42

B

babirusa 2:44
baboon, gelada 2:46
Babyrousa babyrussa **2:**44
baiji **4:**28
Balaenoptera
 B. acutorostrata **10:**50
 B. borealis **10:**54
 B. musculus **10:**40
 B. physalus **10:**42
Balantiocheilos melanopterus **8:**84
Balantiopteryx infusca **2:**64
Balearic Islands **6:**40; **9:**72

Bali **9:**30, 68
Baltic **8:**72; **9:**36
bandicoot
 eastern barred **2:**48
 golden **2:**48
 greater rabbit-eared *1:36*
 little barred **2:**48
 Shark Bay striped **2:**48
 western barred 2:48
Bangladesh **2:**72
banteng 2:50
barb
 bandula 2:52
 seven-striped **5:**82
 various **2:**52
barbet
 toucan 2:54
 various **2:**54
Barbus (Puntius) spp. **2:**52
 B. (P.) bandula **2:**52
bat
 Australian false vampire **2:**56
 ghost 2:56
 gray 2:58
 greater horseshoe 2:60
 greater mouse-eared 2:62
 Guatemalan **2:**62
 Indiana **2:**62
 Kitti's hog-nosed 2:64
 Morris's 2:66
 mouse-tailed **2:**64
 myotis, various **2:**66
 sheath-tailed **2:**64
 see also flying fox
Bawean Island **4:**8
bear
 Asian black **2:**68
 Asiatic black **2:**74
 brown **2:**68
 grizzly 2:68
 Mexican grizzly *1:37*; **2:**68
 polar 2:70
 sloth 2:72
 spectacled 2:74
beaver, Eurasian 2:76
beetle
 blue ground 2:78
 Ciervo scarab **2:**80
 delta green ground **2:**78
 Giuliani's dune scarab **2:**80
 hermit 2:80
 longhorn **6:**44
 scarab **2:**80
behavior studies **1:**85
bellbird
 bare-throated **2:**82
 Chatham Island **5:**54
 three-wattled 2:82
Belontia signata **7:**56
beloribitsa **8:**52
beluga **10:**58
Bering Sea **8:**62
Bermuda **7:**66
bettong, northern **7:**90
Bettongia tropica **7:**90
Bhutan **8:**28; **9:**50
big-game hunting **1:**47; **9:**68

105

Acknowledgments

The authors and publishers would like to thank the following people and organizations: Aquamarines International Pvt. Ltd., Sri Lanka, especially Ananda Pathirana; Aquarist & Pond keeper Magazine, U.K.; BirdLife International (the global partnership of conservation organizations working together in over 100 countries to save birds and their habitats). Special thanks to David Capper; also to Guy Dutson and Alison Stattersfield; Sylvia Clarke (Threatened Wildlife, South Australia); Mark Cocker (writer and birder); David Curran (aquarist specializing in spiny eels, U.K.); Marydele Donnelly (IUCN sea turtle specialist); Svein Fossa (aquatic consultant, Norway); Richard Gibson (Jersey Wildlife Preservation Trust, Channel Islands); Paul Hoskisson (Liverpool John Moores University); Derek Lambert; Pat Lambert (aquarists specializing in freshwater livebearers); Lumbini Aquaria Wayamba Ltd., Sri Lanka, especially Jayantha Ramasinghe and Vibhu Perera; Isolda McGeorge (Chester Zoological Gardens); Dr. James Peron Ross (IUCN crocodile specialist); Zoological Society of London, especially Michael Palmer, Ann Sylph, and the other library staff.

Picture Credits

Abbreviations

AL   Ardea London
BBC   BBC Natural History Unit
BCC   Bruce Coleman Collection
FLPA   Frank Lane Photographic Agency
NHPA Natural History Photographic Agency
OSF   Oxford Scientific Films
PEP   Planet Earth Pictures
b = bottom; **c** = center; **t** = top; **l** = left; **r** = right

Jacket

Ibiza wall lizard, illustration by Denys Ovenden from *Collins Field Guide: Reptiles and Amphibians of Britain and Europe*; Grevy's zebra, Stan Osolinski/Oxford Scientific Films; Florida panther, Lynn M. Stone/BBC Natural History Unit; silver shark, Max Gibbs/Photomax; blue whale, Tui de Roy/Oxford Scientific Films

6–7 E.A. Janes/NHPA; **9** Ken Lucas/PEP; **11** Martyn Chillmaid/OSF; **16** John Hartley/NHPA; **17** T. Whittaker/FLPA; **18–19** Brenda Holcombe/Windrush Photos; **21** P. Morris; **23** Okapia/S. Meyers/OSF; **25** Rod Williams/PEP; **26–27** Andrea Florence/AL; **29** Mark Cawardine/Still Pictures; **31** Owen Newman/OSF; **33** Survival Anglia/Michel Strobing/OSF; **37** Max Gibbs/Photomax; **39** E. Vanderduys; **43** P. Morris; **45** John R. Bracegirdle/PEP; **47** Tobias Bernhard/OSF; **49** Animals Animals/Michael Dick/OSF; **52–53** Tui de Roy/OSF; **55** Daniel Heuclin/NHPA; **56–57** J.L.G. Grande/BCC; **59** Ralph & Daphne Keller/NHPA; **61** Jean-Paul Ferrero/AL; **62–63** Aqualog; **64–65** Mike Hill/OSF; **66–67** Dinodia Picture Agency/S. Nagaraj/OSF; **69** Steve Turner/OSF; **71** Martin Garwood/NHPA; **73** Dr. Robert Franz/PEP; **75t** & **75b** Tony Tilford/OSF; **79** C. Sadler/Natural History New Zealand; **80–81** Steve Littlewood/OSF; **83** Haroldo Palo Jr./NHPA; **85** F.W. Lane/FLPA; **91** Pete Oxford/BBC; **93** Erwin & Peggy Bauer/BCC; **95** A.N.T./NHPA.

Artists

Graham Allen, Norman Arlott, Priscilla Barrett, Trevor Boyer, Ad Cameron, David Dennis, Karen Hiscock, Chloe Talbot Kelly, Mick Loates, Michael Long, Malcolm McGregor, Denys Ovenden, Oxford Illustrators, John Sibbick, Joseph Tomelleri, Dick Twinney, Ian Willis